Chester Railways
the railways of Chester and Saltney
a photographic history

Merseyside Railway History Group

Chester Railways – the railways of Chester and Shotton, a photographic history
First published in Wales in 2015
by
BRIDGE BOOKS
Pear Tree Cottage
The Orchard
Worthenbury
Wrexham County Borough
LL13 0BF

© 2015 Photographs, maps and text, Merseyside Railway History Group
© 2015 Design, typesetting and layout, Bridge Books

All Rights Reserved.
No part of this publication may be reproduced,
stored in a retrieval system, or transmitted
in any form or by any means, electronic,
mechanical, photocopying, recording or
otherwise, without the prior permission
of the Copyright holder.

ISBN 978-1-84494-101-8

A CIP entry for this book is available from the British Library

Cover illustration: An artistic impression of the preserved locomotive (Nº 7822) *Foxcote Manor* crossing the Roodee Bridge at Chester with a train of carmine and cream coaches in the British Railways era. Chester Racecourse can be seen behind the locomotive, with Chester city centre on the skyline. [An original painting by transport artist Derek Roberts]

Printed and bound by
Gutenberg Press Ltd
Malta

Contents

Merseyside Railway History Group	4
Introduction	5
Notes	6
Acknowledgements	7
Historical Background	9
Map 1: Chester & Saltney, 1906	12
Map 2: Chester General Station, 1880s	13
The Crewe line: Waverton–Chester General East End	15
Chester General – a joint station then and now	38
The Birkenhead line: Chester General West End–Mollington	58
The north Wales and Wrexham lines: Chester Nº 6–Balderton	80
The Cheshire Lines Committee – Chester's other station	106
Map 3: Northgate Station, 1899	107
Locomotive Sheds	123
Chester Wagon Works	145
Signal Boxes	146
Bibliography	160

Merseyside Railway History Group

The MRHG was formed in 1977 and is comprised of railway enthusiasts interested in the history of local and national railways from 1830 to the present day. Particular attention has been given to local railways on which the group has published four previous books.

The Hooton to West Kirby Branch Line and the Wirral Way (1982)

Railway Stations of Wirral (1994)

The Last Merseyrail Signal Boxes and Their Heritage, Part 1, The Wirral Line (2004) and *Part 2, The Northern Line* (2006).

The group holds monthly meetings on a variety of railway related topics between September and April. These take place at the United Reformed Church in West Kirby. Further details of the group can be obtained from the Secretary, Richard Kells, 20 Cronton Avenue, Wirral, CH46 3SD.

MRHG books are produced by special sub groups and the group responsible for this publication are Adrian Bodlander, Mark Hambly, Harry Leadbetter, Jon Penn and Dave Southern.

Introduction

The initiative for this publication came from a suggestion at one of the MRHG monthly meetings at West Kirby, shortly after the publication of their last book in 2006. In response to the question as to what would be a suitable subject for their next book, Chester emerged as a popular choice. Indeed it was pointed out that while Chester had featured in books about the lines to north Wales or south towards Shrewsbury, there had never been a book focusing solely on Chester. It took some time for a plan to emerge and the 1906 Railway Clearing House diagram gave the limits of the area to be covered.

While Chester cannot claim to be a major railway centre such as Crewe or York, it nevertheless became a busy centre of rail activity due to the fact that it was part of two major rail routes. The LNWR line from Euston to Holyhead took on extra significance due to the importance of the Irish traffic, particularly as the route of the Irish Mail. The GWR route from London Paddington to Birkenhead Woodside, with onward ferry connections to Liverpool, was that company's main access to north-west England, rivalling the LNWR route to Liverpool Lime Street. Freight traffic was plentiful with trains from Birkenhead Docks, the Wrexham Collieries, Holyhead Harbour and major industries such as John Summers Steelworks at Shotton, plus traffic between all the local yards and sidings.

While it is inevitable that Chester General Station dominates the book due to its size and multiplicity of tracks, the authors have tried to ensure that its smaller neighbour at Northgate has not been overlooked. All aspects of the railway scene have been covered, platforms, goods sheds, loco sheds, signal boxes and even the wagon works, in order to give comprehensive coverage of the railway infrastructure.

Notes

Terminology
When referring to Chester General, West End has been used to refer to where the north Wales/Birkenhead lines join the station while East end refers to the Crewe/Warrington lines

Platform Numbering
The platforms at Chester General have been renumbered on several occasions during its history, which has caused confusion when identifying some locations. As far as possible, the use of numbers has been avoided in favour of more general terms. Where numbers have been used they refer to the number in use at the time the photograph was taken and not necessarily that in current use.

Acknowledgements

The authors are very conscious that the publication of *Chester Railways – a photographic history* would not have been possible without the generous support of a number of a number of people. First and foremost are the photographers who have recorded the railway scene in Chester and its environs from the nineteenth century to the present day. Wherever possible they have been credited individually, but in a number of cases the name of the individual photographer has been lost over time. In these cases the name of the individual or organisation holding the copy of the print or postcard made available to the group has been credited. Particular mention must be made of Dave Giddins, Jon Penn and Ted Lloyd who have allowed access to their extensive collections, without which the book would not have been possible. In addition Richard Maund supplied information about the passenger use of the Chester Northgate avoiding line, and John Dixon provided details of the unusual stop lamp in Saltney Yard.

We would also like to acknowledge the Six Bells Junction website for providing extensive information about enthusiast railtours in the 1960s (www.sixbellsjunction.co.uk).

Additionally several of the authors have previously worked with our publisher, Alister Williams of Bridge Books in Wrexham, and we are grateful for his continued support and encouragement. Finally, thanks must go to the families of the authors who have tolerated numerous meetings in their homes and provided very welcome refreshments.

An etching made in the station's early years showing what would have been the main concourse area. It is interesting to speculate on the role of the elevated structure overlooking the scene, perhaps an early version of an information booth? A lost luggage facility is also provided. Among the standing figures appears to be a constable. [Authors' Collection]

Historical Background

The border city of Chester's role as a transport gateway pre-dates the coming of the railways by two millennia, when Roman shipping navigating the Dee to serve the Roman military and commercial centre of Deva, the harbour of which was on the site now occupied by the Roodee racecourse. In due course Saltney, a short way downstream from the Roodee, became Chester's port and remained a shipbuilding centre and viable commercial port into the railway era.

Historically, Chester's most important role from a transport perspective has been as a staging post on the route between London and Dublin. In the eighteenth century, the port of choice for many travellers to Ireland was Parkgate, on the Wirral bank of the Dee, reached by a turnpike road from Chester. However, in the early nineteenth century, the introduction of steam packet boats sailing from improved harbour facilities at Holyhead, to which the journey from London had been considerably improved by Thomas Telford's road through Shropshire and north Wales, led to Chester's role diminishing, although only temporarily. Engineers and politicians recognised that the new railways would become an integral part of the lines of communication between London and Dublin and that the fastest route would be that which combined the shortest practical sea crossing with the quickest rail journey to the capital. The power of the railways was reinforced in 1839 when Liverpool replaced Holyhead as the port for the mail packet service due to it having a fast direct rail link to the capital. Competing proposals were made involving railways to Porth Dinllaen (on the north coast of the Llŷn peninsula) and to Holyhead, but eventually the Chester & Holyhead Railway, with George Stephenson as engineer, received government endorsement. Construction had progressed sufficiently to allow the Irish Mail from London Euston to begin operating in August 1848 (via Crewe and Chester), although, until the Britannia Bridge was completed in March 1850, the London train terminated at Bangor and road coaches conveyed passengers and mails across the Menai Strait via Telford's suspension bridge to join a connecting train for the short journey across Anglesey.

In the chronology of the development of Britain's railway network, the lines radiating from Chester were completed relatively early. Five of the six 'spokes' for which Chester became the hub were in place by the end of 1850, with the sixth following some twenty-five years later. Although they also handled considerable local traffic, these five lines were first and foremost components of longer routes linking the ports of Holyhead and Birkenhead with London, Birmingham, Manchester and other major centres, over which there was a considerable flow of mail, passenger, parcel and freight traffic in the era before air travel and motorways. In the various struggles for influence and control which took place as the early railway companies consolidated, the majority of Chester's railways became part of either the London & North Western Railway (LNWR) or the Great Western Railway (GWR), or of both of them in the case of those lines which were vested with the Birkenhead Railway Joint Committee (BRJC). This duopoly continued following the 1923 grouping and into the nationalised British Railways era when Chester was one of the points where the Western and London Midland Regions met.

The Cheshire Lines Committee (CLC) and Manchester, Sheffield & Lincolnshire Railway (later the Great Central Railway and LNER) presence in the city was geographically and physically separate to the extent that, prior to the creation of a connection at Mickle Trafford in 1942 to meet wartime needs, in the hypothetical event of needing to work a train between Chester General and Chester Northgate, the traffic inspectors tasked with making the arrangements would have had to consider the pros and cons of sending it via either Wrexham, the Birkenhead dock lines or West Cheshire Junction and Mouldsworth.

The main line nature of Chester's railways meant that the main impact of Dr Beeching's re-shaping of British Railways on the area was the closure of smaller intermediate stations on lines that remained open for through traffic, rather than wholesale line closures. The withdrawal of passenger services to Whitchurch (via Tattenhall Junction) and to Mold and Denbigh pre-dated Beeching. The ability to divert the CLC service into Chester General via Mickle Trafford meant that Chester Northgate could be closed without causing hardship to passengers from mid-Cheshire – in fact they benefited from direct access to connections which previously would have only been possible after a brisk stroll or short taxi ride between stations. However, passengers from stations between Wrexham Central and New Brighton inclusive lost their direct service to Chester, while the remaining intermediate stations between Dee Marsh and Chester Northgate, Sealand and Blacon were closed completely.

As this book was being finalised, Chester's railways entered their 175th year and seem assured of a bright future. Among the services on offer to today's traveller from the city are an hourly service to London Euston, taking just over two hours, and four trains per hour to Liverpool, with Lime Street station being reached in under forty-five minutes. Although no longer the primary influence in shaping the timetable, it is still possible to take the train to Holyhead to connect with a ferry to Ireland, and even to do so on a locomotive-hauled train made up of Mark 3 coaches, a pleasant alternative to the ubiquitous multiple units which provide the vast majority of passenger services on Britain's railways today. Chester is currently served by four of the train operating company franchises – Arriva Trains Wales, Merseyrail, Northern and Virgin Trains – each of which operate trains in their own distinct liveries, which by neat coincidence parallels the situation prior to nationalisation when the passenger rolling stock of all of the 'Big

Four' companies could be seen at Chester on a daily basis. The GWR, LMS and LNER all served the city in their own right, while the green coaches of the Southern Railway appeared on through services between the south coast resorts and Birkenhead which were generally worked forward by the GWR from Reading.

Last, but not least, at Eaton Hall on the outskirts of Chester, on four Sunday afternoons each year, it is uniquely possible to experience the charms of a 15-inch gauge estate railway, laid out according to the principles set out by Sir Arthur Heywood in late Victorian times, travelling in replicas of the original rolling stock hauled by a replica locomotive.

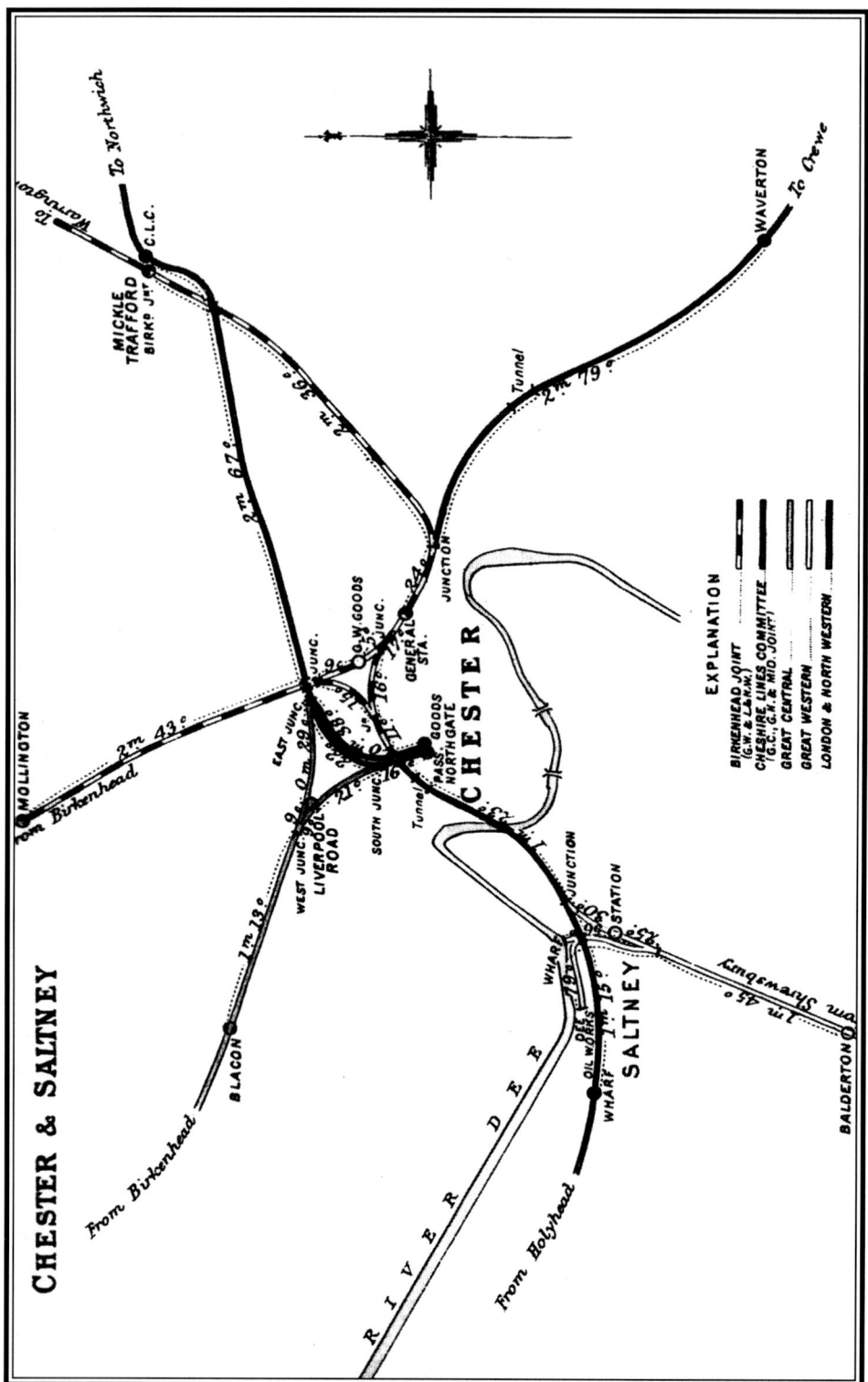

MAP 1
The Railway Clearing House Junction map of 1906, shows the routes of the various railway companies in the Chester area and defines the limits of this publication.

the railways of Chester and Saltney 13

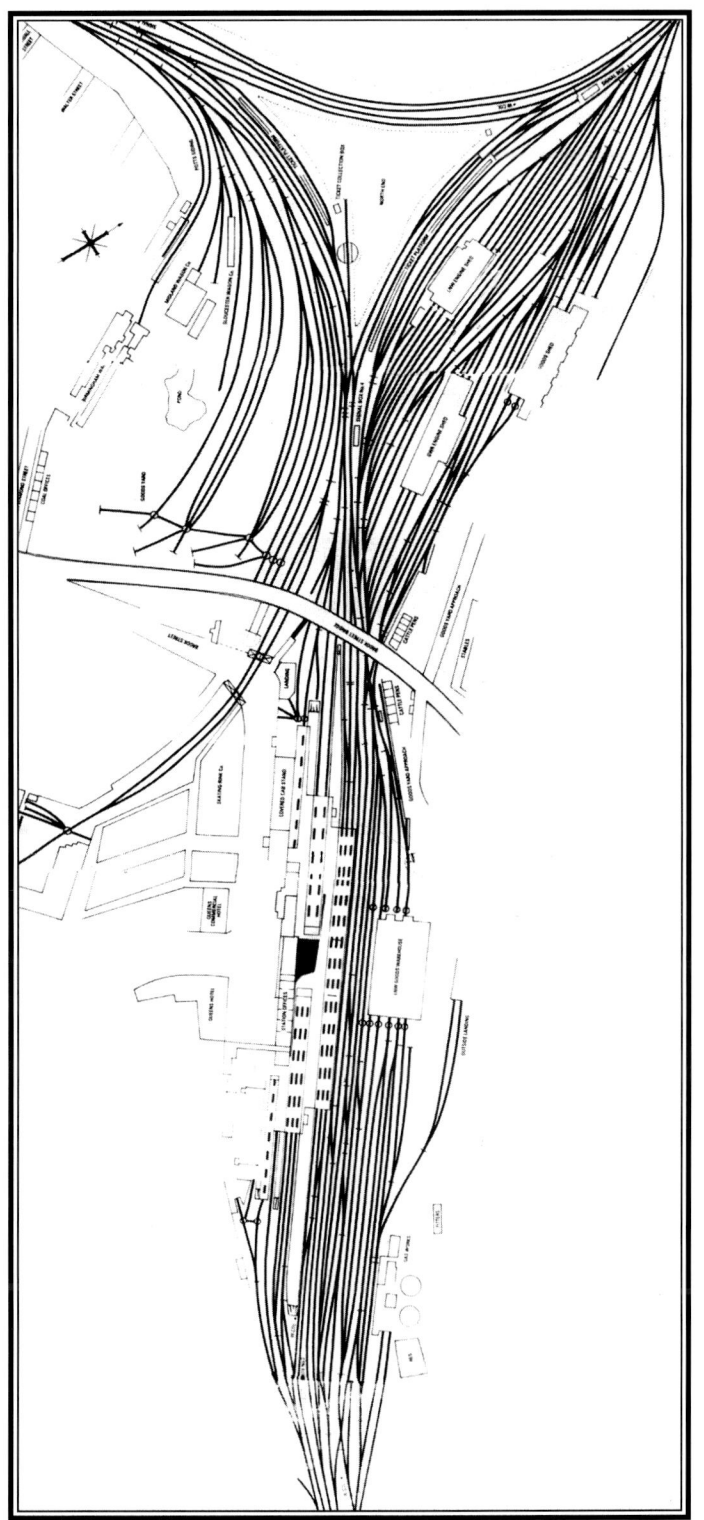

MAP 2
The complexity of tracks in and around Chester General Station is shown in the 1880s before a major enlargement was undertaken in 1890.

The Crewe Line: Waverton–Chester General East End

1. WAVERTON, 1957
A view of the station showing the main building on the Crewe-bound platform with the wooden goods shed behind. The station opened in 1898 and replaced an earlier station which dated from the opening of the line in 1840. The substantial and ornate buildings were at the request of the Duke of Westminster whose estate was nearby and many distinguished visitors would pass through the station en route to visit him. [HB Priestley]

2. CHRISTLETON c1930
Christleton signalbox controlled a crossover on the Crewe side of Christleton tunnel. The tall box was to give the signalman sighting over the tunnel, the very tall signal would be visible to the driver before he entered the tunnel, while the lower arm repeated the upper and would be visible to the driver as he emerged from the tunnel.
[RS Carpenter Collection]

3. CHRISTLETON, c1930
Water troughs were located immediately on the Chester side of the tunnel, and in this view Scot (6117) is passing over them with an express for Holyhead. The gentleman in the mac, with his back to the photographer, is presumably a fellow enthusiast. [RS Carpenter Collection]

4. CHESTER, 1921
LNWR Whitworth 2-4-0 (2157), *Unicorn,* departs Chester with a Whitchurch train. The line to the right is the connection to the LNW shed while visible above the road bridge is the original Chester Nº 1 signal box. [LGRP]

5. CHESTER, 1920
Another Whitworth 2-4-0, this time (732) *Hecla,* heads for Whitchurch with a goods train passing a an unidentified loco on the shed road, while at least one of the railwaymen on the embankment has turned to watch. [LGRP]

6. CHESTER, 1920s
GWR Armstrong Class 4-4-0 (4171) approaches Chester in the mid 1920s with a heavy freight train. [EC Lloyd Collection]

7. CHESTER, 1940s

A superb view of the easterly approach to Chester with the Warrington lines to the left and the Crewe lines to the extreme left. The photograph has been taken from the road bridge seen in the previous photographs while the second Nº 1 signal box, opened in 1958, was built directly in front of where the photographer is standing, adjacent to the crossover pointwork. It is thought this photograph was taken in the late 1940s. [Milepost 92½/AWV Mace Collection]

8. CHESTER N° 2, c1900
An excellent panoramic view of the east end of Chester General at the height of the LNWR period of operation. Immediately to the left of the box a passenger train has departed for Crewe, while on the right a freight is departing for the Warrington line and a further train is shunting the sidings. [EC Lloyd Collection]

9. CHESTER Nº 2, *c*1930s
A heavy express for north Wales passes Nº 2 box double headed by GWR 4-4-0 Bulldog Class (3426) piloting an ex LNWR King George the Fifth Class 4-6-0. [EC Lloyd Collection]

10. CHESTER Nº 2, *c*1960s
In this view the box and track layout are little altered but the LNWR signals have been replaced by BR-style upper quadrants. The skyline shows several modern office blocks. [I Vaughan]

11. CHESTER N° 2, 1970s

A Class 40 hauled parcels train departs for the Warrington line on a sunny day which highlights the unusual feature of N° 2 box, that the front wall of the brick base is curved, while the wooden top is straight and overhangs the base at both ends but not in the centre. [EV Richards]

12. CHESTER EAST END, 1977
Class 52 (D1023) *Western Fusilier* is seen arriving at Chester on 29 January 1977 with the 'Western Memorial' railtour from London Paddington. Note the Warrington/Manchester line joining from the left and the tall signals visible above the bridge on the Crewe line. [D Southern]

13. CHESTER Nº 2, 1977
The box is bathed in late afternoon sunlight as D1023 brings the 'Western Memorial' railtour into Chester. The tour was one of many organised in 1977 to mark the withdrawal of this popular class of locomotive. [D Southern]

14. CHESTER, EAST END, *c*1920
LNW 2-4-0 (5070) *Wheatstone* departs Chester with a local passenger train. [LGRP]

15. CHESTER, 1921
LNWR Trevithick Class 2-2-2 (3020) *Cornwall* passes through Chester on a Holyhead–Crewe directors' special. This locomotive was withdrawn in 1927 and is now preserved as part of the national collection. It is currently on display at Locomotion, Shildon. [LGRP]

16. CHESTER, 1925
LNWR Experiment Class 4-6-0 (1361) *Prospero* passes Chester station with an up goods, while an 0-6-0 saddle tank stands next to the water tank which supplied the water columns in the station. [LGRP]

17. CHESTER EAST END, 1970S
A view from the platform ends, looking towards Nº 2 box with three LNWR bracket signals prominent in the foreground, and a single wagon stabled in the centre siding. [Pacer Archive]

18. CHESTER EAST END, 1970s

This slightly more distant view of N° 2 box shows that some limited modernisation has taken place. On the left of the photograph some BR upper quadrant signals stand alongside their LNW colleagues, while the platforms have gained strip-style light fittings.
[Lens of Sutton]

19. CHESTER EAST END SIGNALS, 1960s
An unidentified Black Five arrives at the down platform with a passenger train, passing a DMU on the Up Through line. [Pacer Archives]

20. CHESTER EAST END SIGNALS, 1960s
Black Five (45004) waits for signals on the Up Through road, while an 8F hauled freight passes on the Down Through. [B Taylor]

21. CHESTER EAST END, 1960s
Black Five (45417) passes the water pump house at the east end of Chester General with a goods train. The train is using the goods lines to the rear of the island platform and is probably bound for Birkenhead docks. [Roger Carpenter Collection]

22. CHESTER EAST END, *c*1948
A number of cattle wagons are seen in sidings at the east end of Chester General. Cattle trains operated between Holyhead and Birkenhead, as well as between Birkenhead and Smithfield market in London. [Milepost 92½]

23. CHESTER EAST END SIGNALS, 1925

An earlier view has LNW Precedent Class 2-4-0 (149) *Mercury* at the east end signals with the water pumping house partly visible to the left, and an unidentified loco near Nº 2 box. [LGRP]

24. CHESTER EAST END SIGNALS, 1967

On 4 March 1967, the publishers Ian Allan ran two special trains between London Paddington and Birkenhead Woodside to mark the end of through trains on that route. One of the trains, called *The Zulu,* was hauled by preserved Castle Class (7029) *Clun Castle*. The loco is seen at the east end of the station.
[D Giddins Collection]

25. CHESTER EAST END, 1960s
Several young train spotters admire ex LMS 2-6-4 tank (42618) as it stands at the at the east end of the down main platform with a passenger train. [J Penn Collection]

26. CHESTER EAST END SIGNALS, 1966
Ex LMS 2-8-0 (48773) waits for the road at the LNWR bracket signal controlling the centre road through the station. A solid-looking cast iron water column is between the loco and the signal. This loco has been preserved and is now based on the Severn Valley Railway. [HC Casserley]

27. CHESTER, CREWE BAYS, 1964
The east end of Chester General station boasted two sets of bay platforms. The down side bays served the Crewe line, while the central bays served the Warrington/Northwich lines. In this view ex LMS 'jinty' (47389) is in the downside bay at the head of a parcels train for Crewe. [Authors' Collection]

28. CHESTER, CREWE BAYS, c1960
A first generation DMU in early BR livery stands in the Crewe platform, while limited modernisation is in progress in the shape of new platform canopies. [Authors' Collection]

29. CHESTER, CREWE BAYS, 1966
Black Five (45295) stands in the centre road of the Crewe bays with a three-coach train. The newly constructed canopies give shelter to some elderly luggage trolleys. [HC Casserley]

30. CHESTER, CREWE BAYS, *c*1980s
A two car Pacer in the distinctive orange livery of the now defunct GMPTE (Greater Manchester Passenger Transport Executive) stands in the Crewe bay. In the background, another unit in the same livery stands at the up main platform. The centre stabling road in the bay has now been lifted. [Authors' Collection]

31. CHESTER, CREWE BAYS, 1985
By complete contrast, preserved GWR 4-6-0 (6960) *Raveningham Hall* stands at the same location during a break while on railtour duty on 10 June 1985 in connection with the 150th anniversary of the GWR. [D Giddins]

32. CHESTER, WHITCHURCH BAY, 1955
Alongside the Crewe bays was a single bay used by trains for Whitchurch. Fairburn tank (42188) is at the head of such a train in December 1955. To the left of the Whitchurch bay is the horse landing, a reminder of the early days of rail travel when rich gentlemen would bring their horses and carriages with them for their onward journeys. [SW Sharpe/D Giddins Collection]

33. CHESTER, MANCHESTER BAYS, c1948
LMS Jubilee Class (5723) *Fearless* departs from one of the Manchester bay platforms with a local service. The angle of the loco and its tender show it is negotiating a particularly severe dip in the track and this, together the rather run-down appearance of the track and buildings, suggests that the photo may have been taken in the immediate post-war period. Close scrutiny of the smokebox number-plate shows that it has been cast with the five-figure BR number, but the first number has been painted out so that only the LMS number is visible, suggesting that some of the staff have not yet accepted the new regime of nationalisation. [J Penn Collection]

34. (FACING) CHESTER, MANCHESTER BAYS RAIL CRASH, 8 MAY 1972
The scene of a major rail crash at Chester General when the 19.31 freight from Ellesmere Port to Mold Junction collided with a stationary passenger train. The train consited of 38 wagons, hauled by Class 24 diesel (5028). The first five wagons were tank wagons containing kerosene, petrol and gas oil. At around 20.50 it approached Chester on a 1 in 100 falling gradient when the driver discovered that the brakes had failed. The train passed a signal at danger and ran into Nº 11 bay platform where it collided with a DMU. The first coach of the DMU was destroyed. The second coach was torn from its bogies and thrown up onto the platform where it demolished the refreshment room wall. Escaping fuel ignited and the station was engulfed in flames. The fire brigade was quickly on the scene and rescued a trapped postal worker and evacuated passengers from a nearby train. There were no fatalities and only minor injuries. Both trains were written off and a section of the station roof had to be removed and has never been replaced. The cause of the accident was traced to the guard of the freight train failing to reconnect the brake pipes after the loco had run round its train at Helsby. The driver had also failed to carry out a brake test. The Class 25 is pushing an empty Park Royal DMU into place to act as a barrier vehicle in case the crashed DMU topples over. [EV Richards]

35. (ABOVE) RAIL CRASH, 1972
A close up view showing the barrier coach in place and the crashed DMU firmly embedded in the platform. [EV Richards]

36. (RIGHT) RAIL CRASH, 1972
After the crash the wrecked loco off the freight train stands among the twisted girders of the station roof showing the intensity of the fire.
[B Hikey/[J Penn Collection]

37. RAIL CRASH, 1972
The leading vehicle of the DMU, which was hit by the freight train, does not look too badly damaged in this view apart from some fire blistered paint work at the cab end. [B Hikey/J Penn Collection]

38. RAIL CRASH, 1972
The loco and one coach of the DMU have been removed to a siding to await their fate. [J Penn Collection]

39. CHESTER, MANCHESTER BAYS, 1999
Class 101 DMU (101678), now in service with First North Western, stands at platform 6 with a train for Manchester Piccadilly. [John Thomas]

40. CHESTER, MANCHESTER BAYS, 1999
The same train is seen from the buffer stops, while the crew have a chat prior to departure. [John Thomas]

Chester General – a joint station then and now

The significance of Chester station to the city it serves and to the national network is emphasised by the fact that it was used by around five million passengers in 2014, one in five of whom arrived, changed trains and continued their journey on another service. As such, in terms of passenger numbers, it is around the 100th busiest station in Great Britain, or around 30th nationally after removing the London termini and other significant, predominantly commuter, stations in the surrounding conurbation.

There has now been a station in the vicinity of Brook Street and City Road for 175 years, and the general layout of today's station would be instantly recognisable to a time traveller from as far back as 125 years ago. The present-day arrangements, with services provided by four different operators, are arguably not unlike those which have prevailed for much of the station's history; different businesses co-existing in varying degrees of harmony, occasionally promoting competing services but for the most part offering the traveller a range of services and connections of varying degrees of convenience and reliability. In fact it might be argued that, over the entire preceding 175 years, the only operator to really have had a monopoly at Chester was the London Midland region of British Rail for the 30 years or so between the integration of former Western Region operations in the mid 1960s (generally considered to have been marked by the cessation of services to London Paddington in 1967) and privatisation in the mid 1990s.

41. CHESTER MAIN BUILDING, 1958
The elaborate station building at Chester was designed by Francis Thompson in the italianate style and opened on 1 August 1848. It was a joint station serving the Chester & Holyhead, the Chester & Crewe, Shrewsbury & Chester, and the Birkenhead railways; each of which, in due course became part of the LNWR or the GWR companies, or both in the case of the line northwards to the Mersey. The construction was entrusted to the well-known contractor Thomas Brassey, a local man, born just a few miles from Chester. The materials used were Staffordshire blue brick and local Storeton sandstone, with slate roofs. The building gained Grade II listed status in 1970. [RM Casserley]

The story of Chester's railways arguably begins with events in nearby south Lancashire in 1830, where the success of the Liverpool & Manchester Railway inspired the business communities across the north west of England and beyond to promote their own schemes to connect their towns and cities by rail, and in the process, create the core of today's national network. The great and good of both Birkenhead and Chester were no exception in that regard and promoted rival schemes to link their respective municipalities. Their inability to collaborate meant that the plans foundered and it was not until 1836 that new proposals surfaced. Once again, there were competing proposals, both of which progressed to the parliamentary bill stage, but common sense prevailed and arbitrators were appointed to weigh up their relative merits and decide which should be built. Following the arbitrators' decision the the Chester & Birkenhead Railway act received royal assent in July 1837. The Chester & Crewe Railway act was passed in the same parliamentary session and the two companies co-operated during the construction of their railways with a view to operating from a joint station in Chester. This was not initially to be, however, as prior to opening the C&CR was taken over by the Grand Junction Railway which viewed the C&BR as a competitor for traffic to and from Liverpool, to which it had been connected via Earlestown and the L&MR since 1838. Therefore, while the C&BR and C&CR opened in September and October 1840 respectively, connecting passengers had to cross between separate stations either side of Brook Street and generally found that 'connection' was a misnomer due to the state of relations between the two companies.

Despite the competition for traffic to Liverpool evident in the frosty relations between the GJR and the C&BR, the biggest prize on offer to the ambitious railway promoter of the early Victorian era was to be the driving force behind whichever scheme would ultimately be backed by Parliament to provide the rail component of the mail route to Ireland. To attempt to put the significance of that decision into a modern context, the reader may wish to see it as the nineteenth-century equivalent of the selection of the HS2 route in the second decade of the twenty-first century. During the 1830s, competing routes had been surveyed and a number of the giants of the period – Brunel, Stephenson and Vignoles to name three – had been associated with rival proposals. Ultimately, it was the scheme to which George Stephenson was engineer, the Chester & Holyhead Railway, which received the all-important backing at Westminster and led to the Chester & Holyhead Railway Act receiving royal assent in July 1844. Construction began the following year and the section from Chester to Saltney Junction was opened in November 1846 to enable the Shrewsbury & Chester Railway, as the North Wales Mineral Railway had become following its amalgamation with the Shrewsbury Oswestry & Chester Junction Railway, to enter the city. Six months later, while an S&CR train was passing over this initial section of the C&HR, one of the spans of the bridge over the river Dee at the Roodee collapsed under the train with the loss of five lives. The bridge was soon rebuilt, but the lessons learned led to a necessary reassessment by Victorian engineers of the use of cast-iron girders. In May 1848 the C&HR began using their own railway as far as Bangor.

While the S&CR and C&HR were under construction, attention turned to the increasingly inadequate station facilities in Chester, which we may recall were the separate termini of the C&BR and C&CR, connected by a through siding. An October 1845 proposal by the S&CR and C&HR led to the necessary Acts being passed in July 1847 and the new station opening in August 1848, in time for the first run of the Irish Mail through from London Euston. At the same time the avoiding line to the west of the station, allowing through traffic between Birkenhead and Shrewsbury, was opened. The personalities associated with the 1848 station were once again a who's who of the era – Robert Stephenson as the consulting engineer, Francis Thompson as the architect and Thomas Brassey as the builder.

Although the joint committee responsible for running the station comprised one director from each of the companies which had funded it, the London & North Western Railway (successor to the Grand Junction Railway, which itself had arrived at Chester through acquisition of the Chester & Crewe Railway), increasingly

42. CHESTER, 1980s
A close-up view of the frontage shows just how impressive the building is and why it is deserving of listed status. [D Giddins Collection]

became the dominant force, reflecting the aggressive character of its general manager, Captain Mark Huish. The L&NWR had unsuccessfully attempted to take over the S&CR and had subsequently seen it align itself with the Shrewsbury & Birmingham Railway, thus creating an alternative route between the west Midlands and Chester, and on to the Mersey over the C&BR (by now part of an enlarged Birkenhead, Lancashire & Cheshire Junction Railway), with ambitions to reach Manchester and Stockport, in competition with the LNWR. Captain Huish therefore embarked on a campaign of what can only be described as blatant harassment of the S&CR, while intimidating the BL&CJR into loosening its relationship with the S&CR and adopting a position of apparent neutrality which in fact meant supporting the L&NWR. Huish's campaign was at its height from late 1849 to late 1850, although he continued to use the BL&CJR as a thorn in the side of the S&CR for several more years, especially as the S&CR had aligned itself with and subsequently became part of the L&NWR's arch-rival, the Great Western Railway.

While the L&NWR's campaign against the S&CR was underway, the BL&CJR's line from Chester to Walton Junction, south of Warrington, opened at the end of 1850 after the BL&CJR had paid the L&NWR for the right to use the final few hundred yards of the Crewe line in order to be able to enter Chester station. The previous year, the Mold Railway had opened between Mold Junction and Mold, with trains running over the C&HR from Chester to Mold Junction. The C&HR took over the Mold Railway in the same year as it opened.

Ultimately, though, the L&NWR realised that commercially it had to come to an accommodation with the

GWR regarding both companies' business in the Chester, Merseyside and Manchester areas, and this was signed in November 1858 following Huish's departure from the L&NWR. The ultimate, and perhaps inevitable, outcome of this agreement was that the L&NWR and GWR jointly took over the operation of the BL&CJR, now renamed the Birkenhead Railway, with effect from the beginning of 1860. The principles of this arrangement continued through the 1923 grouping and it was only with nationalisation at the beginning of 1948 that the Birkenhead Railway ceased to exist as a separate legal entity.

In the same year as it came by its agreement with the GWR the L&NWR also took over the C&HR and so, as 1860 began, Chester's joint station and immediate railway environs settled into a period of relative stability which was to last until nationalisation and even beyond. Some highlights during that period included:

1867 – creation by the L&NWR and GWR of a 'super' joint committee to bring together all their joint interests, including the Birkenhead Joint Traffic Committee and the Chester Joint Station Committee.

1871 – Joint committee considers inadequacies of Chester station. Some improvements made, primarily in terms of staffing.

1874 – Joint committee fails to agree terms with the Cheshire Lines Committee (CLC) for the opening and operation of a junction between the two railways at Mickle Trafford. The two lines would remain unconnected until 1942 when wartime requirements took precedence over any remaining competitive considerations.

1890 – station rebuilt and becomes known as Chester General to distinguish it from the CLC's Chester Northgate.

1893 – powers obtained to quadruple the Chester & Holyhead Railway (west of Chester General towards Saltney Junction) and the Birkenhead Railway throughout. These works went ahead except for the section between Chester and Ledsham.

1912 – revision of station track layout.

1969 – 'Chester General' reverts to 'Chester' following closure of Chester Northgate.

Papers prepared for a visit to Chester of the BR chairman and the general manager of the London Midland Region in the summer of 1969, shortly before the closure of Northgate, offer an interesting internal view of the post-Beeching but ultimately still declining railway. The area manager role at Chester had been created following the amalgamation of the former Chester and Stoke-on-Trent divisions into a larger unit which retained the name of the latter constituent. Integration of the former separate London Midland and Western control offices had been completed in April 1965, meaning that Chester had operational responsibility for routes west and south of Chester as far as Holyhead, Aberystwyth (and Pwllheli), Craven Arms and Wellington (Shropshire).

The area manager was responsible for over 750 staff with the depot superintendent, operating as part of the chief mechanical & electrical engineer's organisation, managing a further 200. In total, 430 of these staff were train crew, all operating from a single signing-on point which had opened fully in November 1968 combining previously separate offices at Chester station and Chester and Mold Junction sheds.

At that time BR's own parcels services and Royal Mail letter and parcels post were still both significant users of the railway. Work to concentrate parcels traffic at key stations had begun as smaller stations closed and in January 1969 new facilities had been opened in an area of surplus bay platforms on the south side at

42 Chester Railways

43. CHESTER MAIN BUILDING, 1998
The only real difference in the forty years between this photograph and Nos 41 & 42, is the increase in the number of motor vehicles parked outside the station building. [John Thomas]

the Crewe end of the station. Traffic from the Mold and Flint areas was by that time being handled by road from Chester and there were plans to serve Birkenhead and the Wirral in the same way. Surplus railway land on the opposite side of Brook Street bridge from the station had been made available to the GPO for the construction of a new sorting office. At the time it was envisaged that it would be linked to the station by overhead conveyor, as were contemporary developments in Liverpool, Manchester and Bristol, but in the event a dedicated roadway running under Brook Street bridge and alongside the passenger car park was laid out instead.

Car parking warranted a full page in the briefing document including noting, in a tone of apparent surprise, the fact that BR's application to demolish part of the station frontage to make space for additional car parking spaces in the former Mold wing had resulted in 'great consternation' and that 'objections were received from numerous Victorian Preservation Societies to our proposals'. The briefing goes on to report that agreement had ultimately been reached with the local authority permitting 'demolition of station front which is not the original building', with permission being granted in May 1969 for 195 spaces which would be completed by early October, thus meeting additional need anticipated to arise following the closure of Chester Northgate.

Comment was also made on the work of the booking and enquiry offices. The former was open continuously, while the latter was open twelve hours per day, between 8am and 8pm, to deal with personal and telephone enquiries at an average of 80 per hour. Ticket sales generated approaching half-a-million pounds in 1968, of which around a third related to travel to and from London. It was noted that the recent saving of a clerical post following a staffing review had reduced the unit cost of issuing a ticket to 10d (4p).

Much has changed over the 45 years since that visit by the chairman. Freight traffic through Chester has undoubtedly reduced dramatically, especially from the early 1990s onwards. Irish Sea Freightliner container traffic from Holyhead ceased in 1991, followed over time by traffic to or from the Courtaulds plant at Flint, Bersham and Point of Ayr collieries, the coal and oil terminals at Llandudno Junction, Trawsfynydd nuclear power station, the cement terminal at Bangor, Associated Octel's plant at Amlwch and Anglesey Aluminium at Holyhead, all of which were once responsible for significant traffic flows. The changing patterns of railway infrastructure maintenance also led to a reduction in the quantity of ballast sourced from Penmaenmawr, while expansion of the pipeline network for the handling of petroleum products led to the eventual cessation of all rail traffic from Stanlow. Three regular freight flows currently pass through Chester Station: the Sellafield-Valley flask traffic for Wylfa nuclear power station, worked by Direct Rail Services; timber from Carlisle to the Kronospan works at Chirk, headed by the distinctive yellow, orange and black locomotives of Colas Rail; and the opencast coal from Ayrshire to the Castle Cement works at Penyffordd, worked by DB Schenker.

The situation with passenger services over the same period has been somewhat different, with definite changes to the patterns of service rather than decline being the more accurate descriptor. The emergence of low-cost air travel and increased private-car ownership during the period have meant that, while services from London, Birmingham and Manchester via Chester to and from Holyhead still provide ferry connections to varying degrees, Anglo-Irish foot passenger traffic has a much reduced bearing on the structure of the timetable. The emphasis is nowadays on more frequent regular interval services, generally formed of relatively short multiple-unit trains. These include through trains between north and south Wales supported by the Welsh Assembly, an hourly service to and from London, and four trains per hour to Liverpool courtesy of Chester's position since 1993 as the southern terminus of Merseyrail's Wirral Line. The latter is arguably a classic example of success breeding success – as service frequency increased it drove up passenger numbers. Following the closure of Birkenhead Woodside in 1967, the service between Chester, Birkenhead and Liverpool was for much of the day an hourly DMU to and from Rock Ferry where passengers changed for a Merseyrail electric service to Liverpool. Upon the initial southward extension of electrification to Hooton in 1985 the Chester DMU connection operated half hourly.

44. CHESTER, 1922
A trio of LNWR engines, including 4-4-0 (1940) closest to the camera stand on the through lines under Chester's overall roof, awaiting their next turns of duty.
[Milepost 92½/AWV Mace Collection]

45. CHESTER, *c*1938
A double-headed passenger train has just arrived at the up main platform, which was numbered 5 at that time. The locos are Watford tank (6894) piloting an unknown Precursor 4-4-0.
[Milepost 92½/AWV Mace Collection]

46. CHESTER, 1950s
Probably an early morning scene as workers await their train. The crossover arrangement here gave flexibility to double platform capacity for shorter local trains. A number of the workers seem to be aware they are being photographed.
[EC Lloyd Collection]

47. CHESTER, 1950s
The same platform, now deserted, photographed in the opposite direction. Note the motorcycle 'packaged' for despatch by rail.
[EC Lloyd Collection]

48. CHESTER, 1950s
A view of the spacious area at the rear of the main building which gave access to an enquiry office, waiting rooms and the station master's office.
[EC Lloyd Collection]

49. CHESTER, 1953
LMS 2P Class 4-4-0 (40628) stands at the down main platform with a train for Rhyl in September 1953.
[Milepost 92½/AWV Mace Collection]

50. CHESTER, 1930s
LMS Black Five (5044) stands at the down main platform, which at that time was numbered platform 4. Shafts of sunlight pick out the train while the large enamel advertisements, wooden station signs and gas lamps all add to the atmosphere. [Stephenson Locomotive Society]

51. CHESTER, 1932
A striking study of LNWR 4-6-0 (5926), *Sir Herbert Walker KCB*, waiting departure from Chester. [LGRP]

the railways of Chester and Saltney 47

52. CHESTER, 1960s
Ivatt Mogul (43024) departs from the down main platform via the scissors crossover which split the platform in two. It is presumably overtaking another train which is out of sight behind the photographer. Note Chester No 3 signal box mounted in the wall above the tender of the loco. The sole purpose of this box was to control these two crossovers. [B Hikey/J Penn Collection]

53. CHESTER, 1966
A good view of the central section of the station showing the building covering the up platforms, with No 3 box perched high in the supporting wall overlooking the two through lines with the main station footbridge behind. The Hoole Road bridge is in the foreground almost directly over the photographer's head. [HC Casserley]

54. CHESTER 1965
Enthusiasts crowd the down platform at Chester as they try to get a glimpse of A4 (60007) *Sir Nigel Gresley* as it takes water with the A4 Preservation Society's Paddington Streamliner railtour of 23 October 1965.
[B Hikey/J Penn Collection]

55. CHESTER 1960s
Royal Scot Class (46152) *The King's Dragoon Guardsman* stands adjacent to the water column on one of the through roads, while at the platform road, Black Five (44681) waits with a passenger train for north Wales.
[John Hobbs]

56. CHESTER, 1960s
An unidentified Black Five passes the same location, light engine, while one of its class mates waits at the platform with a passenger train. An adjacent hand cart is piled high with mail bags waiting to be loaded. [Pacer Archives]

57. CHESTER, 1970s
A Class 40 arrives from the north Wales coast with passenger train of Mark 1 carriages, sporting a mixture of blue/grey and maroon liveries. [Pacer Archives]

58. CHESTER Nº 3A SIGNALBOX, 1963
GWR Hall Class (4990) *Clifton Hall* and an unidentified LMS tank locomotive pass the recently commissioned Nº 3A box. Its LNWR predecessor is in situ behind the Hoole Road footbridge and the LNWR bracket signal is still extant. [B Hikey/[J Penn Collection]

59. CHESTER Nº 3A SIGNALBOX, 1970s
In this later view the scene is less cluttered than the previous photo. The LNWR box has gone, together with the Hoole Road footbridge and the LNWR signals have been replaced by a new gantry adjacent to the signalbox. Class 25 (5270) is passing Nº 3A signalbox on the through goods line with a heavy van train, probably bound for Birkenhead Docks. [Pacer Archives]

60. CHESTER, 1966
Framed by an LNWR bracket signal, LNER Pacific (4472), *Flying Scotsman,* passes through Chester on 4 June 1966, with a Gainsborough Model Railway Society excursion from Lincoln to Llandudno and return. The crew of the Class 40 on the platform road get a grandstand view, while a Class 101 DMU in early livery is visible in the Shrewsbury bay. [Brian Taylor]

61. CHESTER, 1947
LNWR 4-4-0 (25376) is bathed in sunlight as it stands on one of the through lines next to the up and down platforms. A member of the train crew is standing at the rear of the tender, possibly checking the couplings. [HC Casserley]

62. CHESTER, 1960s
Class 9F (92127) passes under Hoole Road footbridge with a coal train for Birkenhead. Note (at the left of the picture) the section of an old coach body in use as a bothy for shunting staff.
[HB Priestly / A Bodlander collection]

63. CHESTER, c1960s
The same location as the previous photo but a lot more to see. BR Standard Class 5 (73040) stands on one of the sidings adjacent to some loaded coal wagons, while LMS 'jinty' tank (47350) stands alongside the unusual LNWR bracket signal. [Paul Lawton Collection]

64. CHESTER, 1959
BR Standard Class 5 (73033) is blowing off steam while waiting to depart with a passenger train for north Wales. The trolleys full of mail bags and piles of railway sleepers, which are partly blocking the far platform would not be acceptable in today's health and safety culture. [HC Casserley]

65. CHESTER, 1998
Two contrasting styles of sign in the centre of Chester station, The top one, giving the mileages to London & Holyhead, dates from the BR London Midland era, while the lower, erected by Railtrack, reflects the privatization which took place in 1994. [John Thomas]

66. CHESTER MIDDLE YARD, 1967

A busy scene reflected the large amount of freight that was still being handled by the railways in the 1960s. All the sidings are full of vans while the goods shed is host to a number of road tractors and trailers. The driver of LMS Black Five (44993) is leaning out of his cab window looking rather bored, while his fireman is standing by the water column. [D Giddins Collection]

67. CHESTER MIDDLE YARD, 1999
Thirty-two years later the scene has altered considerably, with the yard reduced to a few overgrown sidings, playing host to Class 37 (37426) in EWS livery, three tank wagons and a ballast wagon. The new houses to the rear of the loco have been built in the entrance to the former goods yard. Behind the tank wagons the former goods shed still stands, albeit now in private use. [John Thomas]

68. CHESTER, *c*1973
This vehicle has a direct link with two of the authors who were involved with its purchase from BR and subsequent preservation. It was built by the Lancashire & Yorkshire Railway in 1914 as an ambulance carriage. The LMS rebuilt it in 1923 as a medical examination car (10825) in which role it would have toured loco depots round the country to allow the medical officer to carry out routine medical exams of footplate staff. Renumbered DM 45017 by BR, it ended its days at Holyhead, where it was purchased for preservation. It is seen at Chester on route to the Severn Valley Railway in a freight train, with one of the authors on board. It is now in the care of the Museum of Science and Industry in Manchester. [Dave Southern]

69. CHESTER, 1980s
A Class 25 in BR blue livery stands in front of the goods shed which, by this date, had passed to National Carriers Ltd, who were operated as a subsidiary of BR. [Dave Southern]

70. CHESTER, 1980
1980 was the year when the railways celebrated 150 years since the opening of the Liverpool & Manchester Railway, which event was marked by a grand cavalcade of locomotives over the three days of the Spring Bank Holiday at the end of May. The cavalcade took place at Rainhill, scene of the 1829 locomotive trials which was won by *Rocket*. After the event was over, the exhibits returned to their home bases and this photograph, taken on 29 May, shows Class 25 (25272) hauling three preserved locos and three support coaches from Bold Colliery (where the exhibits were stored overnight) to Bridgnorth on the Severn Valley Railway. The three preserved locos were, GWR 2251 Class 0-6-0 (3205), WD Class 2-10-0 (600) *Gordan* and Western Diesel (D1062) *Western Courier*. [D Giddins]

71. CHESTER, 1980
A rear view of the preserved locos waiting at the signal gantry on the through line at the rear of Chester General Station. [D Giddins]

72. CHESTER, 1980s
A Class 31 approaches the colour light signals which replaced the former semaphore signals under the 1984 resignalling. [Dave Southern]

73. CHESTER, *c*1990
An immaculate Class 47 in Inter City livery passes through a gloomy Chester station with the royal train.
[Dave Southern]

The Birkenhead Line: Chester General West End– Mollington

74. CHESTER, DOWN PLATFORM, 1960s
Ex LMS Fairburn tank (42235) waits for the road in a typical steam era scene, with LNWR bracket signals to the left and water columns to the right. Some modernisation is evident in the modern canopies and the cast iron platform lights are in the process of being replaced with a more modern design.
[Brian Taylor]

75. CHESTER, DOWN PLATFORM, 1960s
The fireman uses one of his fire irons to hold the 'bag' in for Stanier 2-6-4 tank (42613) of Birkenhead shed as it takes water from a very leaky water column. The clean state of the loco and the white painted buffers indicate that it is probably being prepared for railtour duty.
[Brian Taylor]

76. CHESTER, BIRKENHEAD BAY, 1960s
A BR Standard Class 4 2-6-0 takes water in the Birkenhead bay. Some colour light signals have replaced the elderly LNWR signals at this location. [Brian Taylor]

77. CHESTER, WEST END, 1966
This panoramic view clearly show the complex trackwork at the West end of Chester General Station. Ex LNER Pacific (60532) *Blue Peter* runs tender first through the station in connection with a railtour working while an unidentified Class 40 waits at the platform. [Brian Taylor]

78. CHESTER, Nº 3A SIGNAL BOX, 1966
A close-up view of *Blue Peter* as it passes Nº 3A signalbox. The railtour was the Altincham Railway Excursion Society's Holyhead and Brymbo Special of 21 August 1966. [Brian Taylor]

79. CHESTER, Nº 3A SIGNAL BOX, 1960s
Ivatt Mogul (46509) passes Nº 3A box light engine, on one of the central through lines. The Hoole Road footbridge in the background has lost some sections of its roof. [DJ Montgomery/D Giddins Collection]

80. CHESTER, Nº 3A SIGNAL BOX, 1967
Preserved GWR Castle Class (4079), *Pendennis Castle*, is seen passing Nº 3A signalbox on 4 March 1967 having worked one of two special trains to commemorate the end of through services between London Paddington and Birkenhead Woodside. Its partner (7029), *Clun Castle*, has already been seen at the east end of the station. [D Giddins Collection]

81. CHESTER, BIRKENHEAD BAY, 1960s
Ex GWR Pannier tank (9752) basks in the sun as it stands in the Birkenhead bay platform. Note the new platform canopies being installed. [MEM Lloyd]

82. CHESTER, BIRKENHEAD BAY, 1960s
Class 47 (D1716) in two-tone green livery stands at the same location as the previous photograph. Chester Nº 4 signalbox is visible beyond the footbridge. [Pacer Archives]

83. CHESTER, WEST END, 1963
A busy scene in the summer of 1963 as Jubilee (45697) *Achilles* pilots rebuilt Scot (46148) *The Manchester Regiment* on a heavy express from the north Wales coast. Partly hidden by the water tower are an LMS 2-6-4 tank and a BR Standard 4-6-0. [GW Sharpe]

84. CHESTER, WEST END, 1940s

An earlier scene at the same location as the previous photograph shows LNWR 4-4-0 (5404), *Colwyn Bay*, arriving from north Wales.
[D Giddins Collection]

85. CHESTER, WEST END, 1960s

An oil tank train from Stanlow refinery arrives off the line from Birkenhead behind GWR 2-8-0 (3861). The brake van behind the loco acts as a barrier vehicle, while a Crosville bus is visible on the road bridge in the background.
[B Hikey/[J Penn Collection]

86. CHESTER, WEST END, 1954

Black Five (45015) passing the GWR shed on 10 July 1954 with the 09.25 Llandudno–Leamington train. Prominent on the shed is GWR Mogul (6317).
[DJ Montgomery/
D Giddins Collection]

87. CHESTER Nº 4, 1960s
Black Five 4-6-0 (44776) arrives at Chester with a passenger train passing under the LNWR signal gantry.
[B Hikey/J Penn Collection]

88. CHESTER Nº 3A, 1960s
Ex LNER B1 Class (61313) passes under Hoole Road footbridge with a special off the Eastern Region. The small headboard indicating it is probably hauling an enthusiast's railtour. Edward Thompson, the loco's designer was the grandson of Francis Thompson who designed the station building.
[B Hikey/J Penn Collection]

89. CHESTER Nº 3A, 1960s

A former Crosti-boilered 9F 2-10-0 passes the same location as the previous photo with a van train.
[B Hikey / J Penn Collection]

90. CHESTER, 1960s

Class 40 (D287) in early BR livery with small yellow warning panel stands at the down platform with a train of Mark 1 stock. Note the Hoole Road footbridge passing over the first coach.
[Authors' Collection]

91. CHESTER, 1970s

Class 40 (40185) in BR Blue with corporate logo, gets the road from one of the LNWR bracket signals. Chester Nº 6 signalbox is visible on the right.
[Authors' Collection]

92. CHESTER, SHREWSBURY PLATFORM, c1910
GWR 4-4-0 Duke Class (3269), *Dartmoor*, stands at platform 1, which was the usual platform for Shrewsbury trains at this time. The LNWR train in platform 1A behind the wall was probably a local for Denbigh or Rhyl. It is worth noting that the footplate man oiling the loco appears to be wearing a bowler hat. [J Thomas Collection]

93. CHESTER, BIRKENHEAD BAY, c1947
LMS Fairburn 2-6-4 tank (2263) waits departure amongst the clutter surrounding the Birkenhead Bay. Note the pile of ash in front of the loco were numerous engines have had their fires cleaned. [Milepost 92½]

94. CHESTER, BIRKENHEAD BAY, 1964
Fairburn Tank (42202) with a train for Birkenhead. Note the wooden huts used by the track gang and the empty luggage barrows on the platform. The overall roof at this end of the station has now been removed and replaced by modern platform canopies. [HC Casserley]

95. CHESTER, WEST END BAYS, c1962
Fairburn tank (42061) has just arrived with a Ruthin–Chester local train. The massive brick columns of the original roof supports contrasting with the modern canopies next to the train. [Paul Lawton Collection]

96. CHESTER, DENBIGH BAY, 1962
On 28 April 1962, a BR Standard Class 4 (75033) waits to depart with the 20.50 train to Ruthin which was the last passenger train on the Mold–Denbigh line. [Brian Cowlishaw/Paul Lawton Collection]

97. CHESTER, Nº 2 PLATFORM, *c*1920
This photograph shows the Birkenhead platform with two sidings and engine release crossovers. The Shrewsbury and Denbigh bays are beyond the brick columns to the left. [EC Lloyd Collection]

98. CHESTER, WEST END, *c*1950
The gloom of this end of the station is well illustrated in this photograph taken from the up main platform looking across to the bay platforms. [EC Lloyd Collection]

99. CHESTER Nº 2 PLATFORM, 1967

In July 1967, Chester held a Festival of the Arts, which included an exhibition at Chester General Station. Preserved LNER Pacific *Sir Nigel Gresley* and AC Electric locomotive (E3036) are seen at platform 2 at the west end of the station. The *Flying Scotsman* (4472) was also part of the exhibition and operated an excursion to Blackpool. B Hikey / J Penn Collection]

100. CHESTER, Nº 2 PLATFORM, 1953
Fourteen years earlier ex-Caledonian Railway 4-2-2 (123) stands at the same location as part of another exhibition, the reason for this one is not known, but is probably connected with the fact that it was Coronation year. [HC Casserley]

101. CHESTER, FORMER BIRKENHEAD BAY, 2004
Forty years have seen a dramatic change to this part of the station. The closure of the Mold–Denbigh line and changing traffic patterns have seen the removal of two of the three bay platforms and the land they occupied being converted to a car park. The remaining bay platform is now used for Shrewsbury services, while the Birkenhead services have been transferred to the north side of the station and from 1994 they were converted to third rail electric operation. On 19 May 2004 a single unit (153321) occupies the Shrewsbury platform.
[John Thomas]

102. CHESTER, WEST END, 1920s
LNWR 4-4-0 (60) passes a siding full of loaded wagons as it arrives at Chester with a passenger train. [Robert Humm]

103. CHESTER Nº 4, 1924
A superb panoramic view of the West End of Chester General station. The sidings in the foreground are filled with various types of early carriages while Nº 4 signalbox, with its adjacent signal gantry, is centre stage. An unidentified LNWR 4-6-0 departs past the GWR steam shed with a freight, while GWR 2-4-0 (3201) is on a van train in the sidings. [Milepost 92½]

the railways of Chester and Saltney 73

104. CHESTER, WEST END, 1920s
Churchward Mogul (4348) heads a Class F fast goods train past the GWR shed in the 1920s. [EC Lloyd Collection]

105. CHESTER No 4, 1960s

A slightly less busy scene as the number of carriage sidings has been reduced and several scruffy sheds have sprung up. A BR Standard loco is at the head of some empty carriages, while Stanier tank (42086) passes on the main line. The steam shed has been converted for use by DMUs. [Roger Carpenter Collection]

106. CHESTER Nº 4, 1920s
GWR Mogul (4350) leaves Chester with a passenger train, which is formed mostly of clerestory coaches. [LGRP]

107. CHESTER Nº 4, c1930
Royal Scot (6162) makes a spirited departure for north Wales passing under the superb display of LNWR signals with Nº 4 box in the background. [EC Lloyd Collection]

108. CHESTER, WEST END, *c*1995
Departmental railcar (960001) enters Chester in 1995. This was originally a Class 121 single-unit railcar, which was converted to a track recording vehicle by Balfour Beatty, who operated it for Railtrack. Note the simplified track layout and colour light signals, in contrast with earlier views. [Dave Hill]

109. CHESTER Nº 5, 1970s
Class 24 (24082) and a sister engine adjacent to Nº 5 Box on the Birkenhead line. The avoiding line is visible behind the locos while the overbridge carried the former CLC line to Chester Northgate. [Ivor Martindale]

110. CHESTER Nº 5, 1972
On Sunday, 4 June 1972, Class 50 (50039), *Implacable* (carrying its earlier number of '439') reverses a diverted west coast main-line train round the avoiding line. These trains became a common sight on Sundays in the early 1970s as work to electrify the west-coast line between Crewe and Glasgow meant trains between Liverpool and London had to be diverted via Chester. The Birkenhead lines are in the centre, curving past Nº 5 signalbox, while the DMU is entering the diesel depot. [EV Richards]

111. BACHE, 1985
A view of Bache looking towards Birkenhead, with the platforms dwarfed by the large supermarket building on the left. The GWR opened a goods yard on this site in 1911 and it survived until 1969 for general goods and 1972 for coal. The increase in house building near the site led to the decision to build a new station to replace the one at Upton-by-Chester. The redevelopment was a joint project between the supermarket chain and British Rail. [ND Mundy/EC Lloyd Collection]

112. UPTON-BY-CHESTER, 1950s
A Class 4F 0-6-0 goods engine, passes through Upton-by-Chester with a mixed freight. This station on the Birkenhead–Chester line was opened in 1939 as Upton-by-Chester Halt to serve this growing village on the outskirts of Chester. The suffix 'Halt' was dropped from the name in 1968, and the station closed in 1984 when it was replaced by a new station at Bache, 700 metres nearer Chester. [HB Priestley/Pacer Archives]

113. MOLLINGTON, 1957
Ex GWR Pannier tank (3630) passes through Mollington with a short freight on 4 November 1957. Mollington was one of the original stations on the line being opened by the Chester and Birkenhead Railway on 23 September 1840. It closed to passengers on 7 March 1960 and to goods on 4 January 1965.
[HB Priestly/Pacer Archives]

114. MOLLINGTON SIGNAL BOX, *c*1960s
In this wintery view Mollington signal-box is seen to good effect against the grey sky. The box was opened in 1940 to control some new sidings provided for oil-tank trains and was of the ARP (Air Raid Precaution) design. These boxes featured 14-inch thick brick walls and a 12-inch thick concrete roof which were intended to resist the effect of nearby bomb blasts though not a direct hit. The box closed on 12 November 1980.
[T Bagley/J Penn Collection]

The North Wales and Wrexham Lines: Chester Nº 6–Balderton

115. CHESTER, TUNNEL JUNCTION, 1930s

An unidentified LNWR Prince of Wales Class 4-6-0 departs Chester with a relief Irish Mail working to Holyhead. The tracks to the right were mostly carriage sidings which have long since disappeared, while on the left of the locomotive are the two double-track avoiding lines which connected to the Birkenhead line, only one of which now survives. Even further left are some horse boxes stored in sidings which follow the alignment of the avoiding lines. [Real Photographs]

the railways of Chester and Saltney 81

116. CHESTER Nº 6, 1930s
Royal Scot Class (6146), *Jenny Lind*, passes Nº 6 box with a Holyhead–Euston express. This locomotive was renamed *The Rifle Brigade* in 1936. [J Ryan Collection]

117. CHESTER N° 6, 1949

LMS compound 4-4-0 (41119) makes a spirited departure past N° 6 box with a train for north Wales. Resplendent in its new British Railways livery, this loco was the last of a class introduced in 1924 as a modified version of the earlier Midland railway design.
[Lens of Sutton]

118. CHESTER Nº 6, 1920
Bulldog (3410) *Colombia* passes the box with the down Zulu from Paddington–Birkenhead Woodside. The locomotive on the right is an LNWR Special tank. [HG Tidey/EC Lloyd collection]

119. CHESTER Nº 6, TUNNEL JUNCTION, 1949
Black Five (45292) passes Chester Nº 6 signal box. Tunnel Junction, in the foreground, was the point where the Chester avoiding line joined the north Wales line, allowing trains from the Birkenhead direction to access the latter without reversing in Chester station. [Lens of Sutton]

120. TUNNEL JUNCTION, 1950s
A GWR 2-8-0 (3827) comes off the down avoiding lines with a van train from Birkenhead docks. [D Giddins Collection]

121. TUNNEL JUNCTION, 1949
GWR 4-6-0 (2915), *Saint Bartholomew*, passes one of Nº 6's distinctive LNWR bracket signals as it approaches Chester with a Western Region express. [Lens of Sutton]

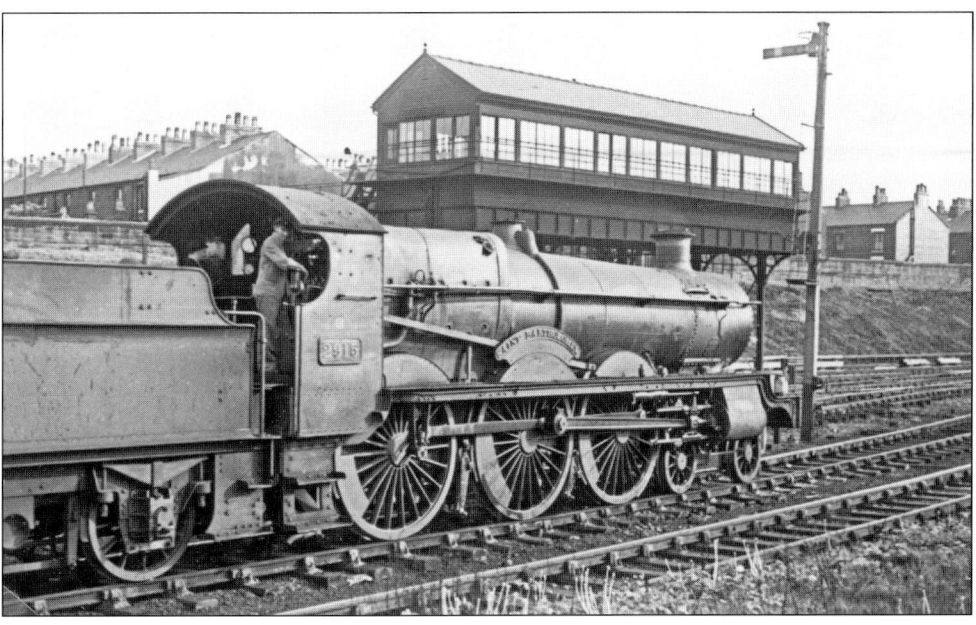

122. CHESTER Nº 6, 1949
After coming off its train and turning on the triangle, *Saint Bartholomew* stands on the avoiding line adjacent to Nº 6 box waiting to take up its next turn of duty. [Lens of Sutton]

123. TUNNEL JUNCTION, 1981
This DMU became derailed on point work while approaching the station with a Wolverhampton–Chester service on 9 June 1981. It then hit a cable bridge with had recently been erected in connection with the Chester re-signalling scheme. Fortunately there were no serious injuries. The accident report showed that the derailment had been caused by a combination of electrical faults on the signalling system and signalman's error. [D Giddins Collection]

124. TUNNEL JUNCTION, 1949
An unidentified Compound 4-4-0 departs with a local passenger train to north Wales. [Lens of Sutton]

125. NORTHGATE STREET TUNNEL, 1960s
An LMS Black Five is about to enter Northgate Street tunnel with a Birkenhead–Smithfield cattle train. In GWR days this train was called 'The Meat'. [Milepost 92½]

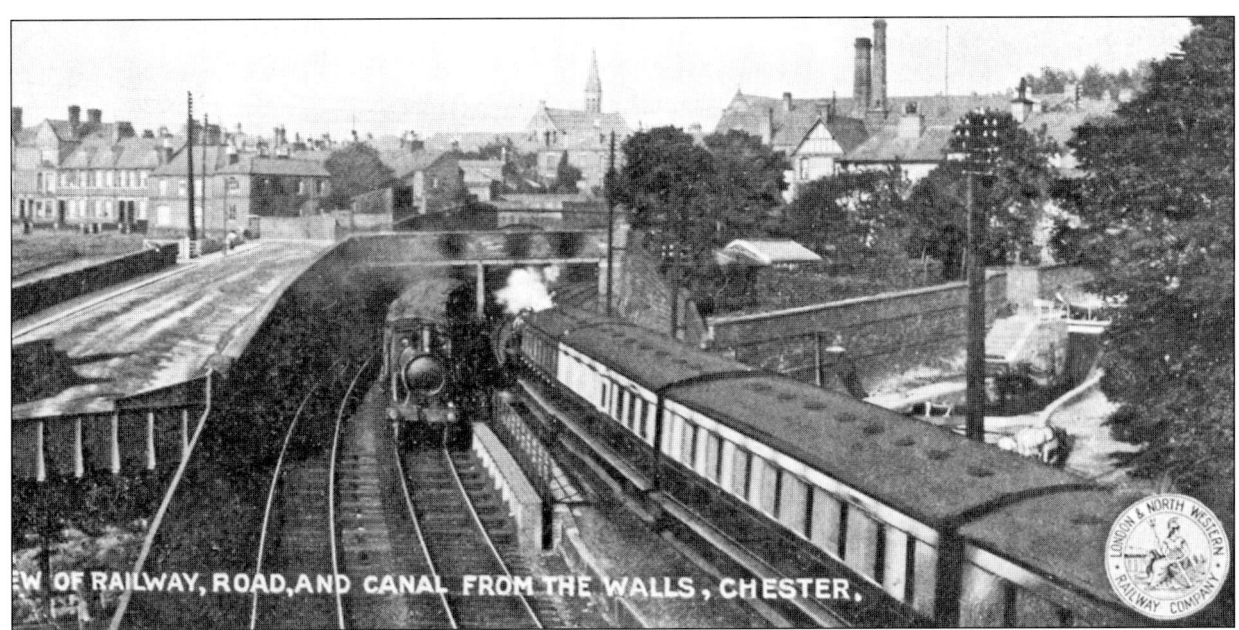

126. NORTHGATE LOCKS, 1905
This official LNWR postcard shows two trains passing on the bridge over the Shropshire Union canal. The locks lifted boats from the level of the River Dee to the canal basin. [HJ Leadbetter Collection]

127. NORTHGATE LOCKS, 1950s
GWR 2-8-0 (3861) crosses Northgate locks with an oil tank train from Stanlow refinery, passing a mixed freight heading towards Chester. [D Giddins Collection]

128. NORTHGATE LOCKS, 1988
Class 47 (47002) waits at the signal near Northgate locks with an engineers' train in this view from the diesel era. [Pacer Archives]

129. CRANE STREET, c1960
An unidentified 78000 Class 2-6-0 approaches Chester with a local passenger train off the Denbigh line. The small signal box in the background is Crane Street, a break-section box which survived until 1967. [Derek Cross]

130. CRANE STREET SIGNALBOX, 1960s
A close up of the box showing its all wood construction and diminutive size which housed just fifteen levers.
[T Bagley/J Penn Collection]

131. ROODEE BRIDGE, c1935
LNWR 4-4-0 (25348), *Coronation*, has just come off the Roodee Bridge with a Rhyl–Chester local train. Prominent features next to the line are the large gas holder and the Crosville motor bus depot.
[Milepost 92½/AWV Mace Collection]

132. ROODEE BRIDGE, c1947
Photographed at the same location as the previous picture, LMS Black Five (5278) approaches Chester with a horse-box special from Holyhead. The race horses would have been brought from Ireland to take part in a meeting at Chester. [Milepost 92½]

133. ROODEE BRIDGE, 1950s
A Black Five (45185) crosses the Roodee Bridge with a north Wales coast express. The gas holder again dominates the scene while the race course is just visible on the right of the picture. [Milepost 92½]

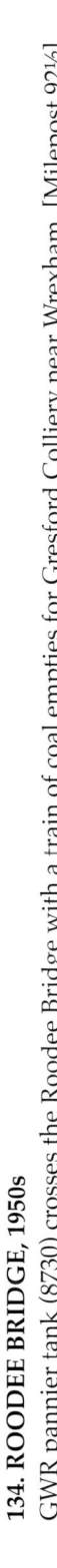

134. ROODEE BRIDGE, 1950s
GWR pannier tank (8730) crosses the Roodee Bridge with a train of coal empties for Gresford Colliery near Wrexham. [Milepost 92½]

135. ROODEE BRIDGE, 1964
A busy scene as an 8F (48672) crosses with an empty tank train for Stanlow, pasing an unidentified Black Five with a mixed freight. The pedestrian walkway at the side of the bridge, with its wooden approaches, is a notable feature. [JA Peden]

136. ROODEE BRIDGE, 1980s
Two-car sprinter unit (150141) crosses the bridge with a local service to Chester. Rationalisation has seen the four tracks reduced to two, with all services now using the former GWR tracks. There appears to be a caravan rally taking place on the racecourse, while a pedestrian has crossed the river on the footpath at the right of the bridge. [D Southern]

137. ROODEE BRIDGE, 1932
An unidentified Midland 4F 0-6-0 has just come off the Roodee Bridge with a short local train, probably heading to the Denbigh line. [WH Whitworth/EC Lloyd Collection]

138. ROODEE BRIDGE, 1970s
Class 40 (40131) heads a Freightliner train for Holyhead before the four-track formation was reduced to two. [D Giddins collection]

139. ROODEE BRIDGE, 1983
Class 56 (56053) has just come off the bridge while heading the 09.23 Fiddler's Ferry–Llandudno Junction fly-ash train. Fly ash, a waste product produced at coal-burning power stations, was used as a construction material in the project to convert the A55 road to a dual carriageway.
[AO Wynn]

140. SALTNEY CUTTING, 1930s
An unidentified LNWR 18-inch 'Cauliflower' Class locomotive heads towards Chester with a three-coach local train.
[WH Whitworth/EC Lloyd Collection]

141. SALTNEY CUTTING, 1932
L&YR-designed 'Crab' Class 2-6-0 (13010) is in charge of an express off the north Wales coast on 12 August 1932.
[WH Whitworth/EC Lloyd Collection]

142. SALTNEY CUTTING, 1962
Rebuilt Royal Scot (46132) *The King's Regiment Liverpool*, working the up Emerald Isle express from Holyhead to Euston, is about to pass Black Five (45558) on the down line with a Liverpool–Llandudno service.
[Derek Cross]

143. SALTNEY CUTTING, 1980s
An unknown Class 47 heads a London bound train in this view from the diesel era. A few coaches in the new Inter City livery break the monopoly of the blue and grey. [Pacer Archives]

144. SALTNEY JUNCTION, 1950s
A three-coach auto train operated by an unknown Pannier tank, forms a Wrexham–Chester train in the early 1950s. [Milepost 92½]

145. SALTNEY JUNCTION, c1935
0-6-0 (2572) heads for Chester with a local train off the Wrexham line. [Milepost 92½/AWV Mace Collection]

146. SALTNEY JUNCTION, 1930s
LNWR 0-8-0 (8921) has just passed the junction with a Llandudno Junction–Chester goods working. [Milepost 92½]

147. SALTNEY JUNCTION, 1960s
A three-car DMU passes Saltney Junction box with a local train off the Great Western line. The white cab roofs were a feature of units operated by the Western Region of BR during this period. [Pacer Archives]

148. SALTNEY JUNCTION SIGNALBOX, 1955
Collett 0-4-2T (1416) passes the box in charge of a two-coach auto train for Oswestry in November 1955. [SD Wainwright]

149. SALTNEY STATION, *c*1910
A train of clerestory coaches stand in the down platform of Saltney station. The all-timber built station was opened in 1846 and closed in 1916 as an economy measure during the First World War. A new station was opened by the GWR in 1932. [Lens of Sutton]

150. SALTNEY STATION, 1957
This view shows the second station looking towards Chester. There is a pagoda-style building on the down platform, while a wooden shelter suffices on the staggered up platform. [HB Priestley]

151. SALTNEY, DEE JUNCTION, 1958
Hall Class (6964), *Thornbridge Hall*, passes Saltney yard with an up local train, probably for Shrewsbury or Wolverhampton. Note the impressive telegraph post behind the train. [JA Pedan]

152. SALTNEY, DEE JUNCTION, 1959
A fine collection of lower quadrant signals guard the entrance and exit of Saltney Dee Junction Yard looking towards Wrexham. [PJ Garland]

153. SALTNEY, DEE BRANCH, 1959
The short goods line from Saltney yard to the wharf crossed Saltney High Street on the level before passing under the Chester–Holyhead mainline, where a DMU can be seen on the steel girder bridge. [PJ Garland]

154. SALTNEY, DEE BRANCH, 1957
A view taken from the footbridge in the previous photograph. The branch split at this point; the line under the right hand opening of the bridge leading to the wharf, while the line on the left turned along the river bank to serve various factories. [CHA Townley/J Thomas Collection]

155. SALTNEY WHARF, *c*1880
A very early view of the wharf showing a fine collection of sailing ships waiting to load coal from the railway wagons on the right. An early locomotive is just visible in the centre right of the photo. [J Thomas Collection]

156. SALTNEY YARD, *c*1965
A view of the yard from the south end looking towards Chester. The signals are worked from Green Lane Crossing signal box which is behind the photographer. [PJ Garland]

157. SALTNEY YARD, 1959
This unusual stop lamp was used to prevent conflicting movements between the Back Road and Garden siding and could only be passed on the authority of a shunter. The modern-day equivalent would be a stop and await instructions board. [PJ Garland]

158. GREEN LANE, c1965
In this view we are looking towards Wrexham with Green Lane's crossover in the foreground and its impressive bracket signal to the right. The tall arm applies to the main line, with Saltney Dee Junction's distant below, while the two short arms control the entrance to the down goods loops. [PJ Garland]

159. GREEN LANE LEVEL CROSSING, *c*1965
A view of the signal box and level crossing taken from the up side of the line. The brake vans visible beyond the box are standing on the down goods loop. [PJ Garland]

160. BALDERTON STATION, *c*1950
This small station was opened by the GWR in 1901 and closed by BR in 1952. In this view, looking towards Chester, it is worth noting the contrasting styles of canopy on the two buildings. [Stations UK]

161. BALDERTON LEVEL CROSSING, C1965
By the time this photograph was taken Balderton signal box just controlled the level crossing but, until 1954, it had also controlled a small goods yard which was on the Wrexham side of the crossing on the up side of the line.
[PJ Garland]

The Cheshire Lines Committee – Chester's other railway

The Cheshire Lines Committee (CLC) came into being in the late 1850s as a collaborative effort between three railway companies – the Manchester, Sheffield & Lincolnshire (MS&L), the Midland and the Great Northern – to break the domination of the LNWR in the area around Stockport. The CLC ultimately operated a network of around 140 route miles in north Cheshire and south Lancashire, and was the last of the major British joint railways to retain a separate management structure and visible identity, remaining a distinct operation until becoming part of the London Midland Region of British Railways at nationalisation.

The CLC reached Chester in the mid-1870s, with goods traffic commencing in November 1874 and passenger services six months later, in May 1875, as the culmination of a series of westward extensions across north Cheshire, with Knutsford having been reached in 1862, Northwich in 1863 and Helsby in 1869. The CLC's route to Chester left the Helsby line at Mouldsworth and continued westwards via an intermediate station serving the villages of Barrow and Tarvin to Mickle Trafford where the Chester to Warrington section of the Birkenhead Joint was crossed and a station was provided. Although a physical connection between the two railways at this point was planned, an agreement could not be reached and it was almost seventy years later, when the wartime need to improve access to and from Birkenhead docks, led to a connection being opened in the autumn of 1942 allowing trains from Warrington to join the CLC towards Chester. Beyond Mickle Trafford the CLC route continued westwards before then swinging south to cross the Birkenhead section of the Joint and terminate at a modest terminus at Chester Northgate, a few hundred yards as the crow flies from Chester General.

For Sir Edward Watkin, chairman of the MS&L, the CLC's arrival in Chester provided the means for the MS&L to reach the industrialised north-east corner of Wales around Wrexham and Buckley, not least to supply Denbighshire coal to fuel the rapidly expanding chemical industry at Northwich. The MS&L's route to Wales headed westwards from Chester, with intermediate stations at Blacon and Saughall, until turning through ninety degrees to cross the Dee on the impressive three-span Hawarden Bridge in order to make an end-on junction with the the Wrexham, Mold & Connah's Quay (WM&CQ) Railway's northward extension from Buckley Junction at Shotton. The bridge was declared open by Catherine Glynne Gladstone, wife of the former and future Prime Minister WE Gladstone, at the beginning of August 1889 but the WM&CQ's extension was not finally completed and available for through trains between Chester and Wrexham until the end of March 1890. At that time the WM&CQ and MS&L agreed jointly to take up powers to build the North Wales & Liverpool Railway from Hawarden Bridge – a case of a location taking its name from a structure – through the Wirral Peninsula to Bidston, where a junction was made with the Wirral Railway. By the time that construction was complete and the line opened in March 1896, the WM&CQ had effectively become a subsidiary of the MS&L, although initially only the WM&CQ had running powers beyond Bidston to the Wirral Railway's Seacombe station (for ferry connections to Liverpool) and so initially through services were worked by MS&L locomotives wearing WM&CQ titles and numbers.

At Chester, the works resulted in the creation of a triangular junction just to the north of Chester Northgate, thus enabling through traffic to and from Wales to avoid the terminus, while passenger services to Wrexham (and subsequently the Wirral) used Northgate station, for which the CLC received payment from its shareholder. At the western vertex of the triangle the MS&L built their own station, Chester Liverpool Road, with platforms on both the avoiding line and the curve to Northgate. While Liverpool Road became an established calling point on services from Northgate to and from Wales and the Wirral, apart from a series of summer-only through workings in the early years of the twentieth century to Aberystwyth (via Wrexham, Ellesmere and Oswestry) from Manchester and beyond, and the occasional call by an excursion train, the avoiding lines platforms very rarely saw anything other than passing freight trains. Liverpool Road's close proximity to Northgate ultimately led to its closure to passengers in December 1951 although the goods yard remained open until April 1965.

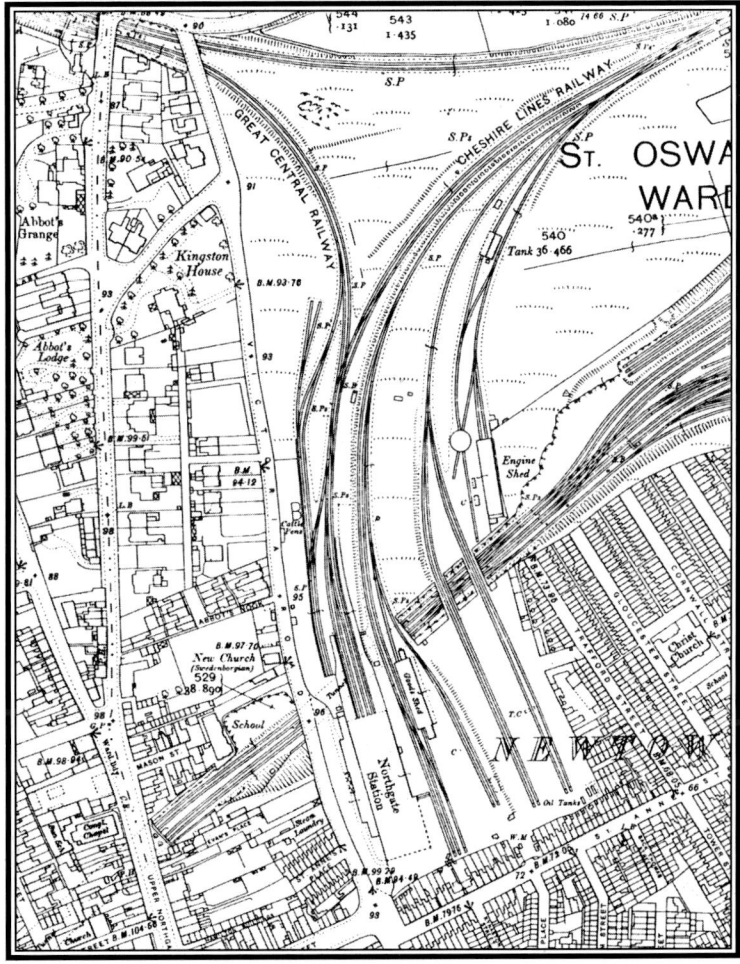

MAP 3
This 1899 map shows Northgate Station and its approach tracks crossing the north Wales coast line, which passes beneath in tunnel. Some of the tracks for Chester General are seen middle right, while Liverpool Road Station was in the extreme top left corner.

108   Chester Railways

   Passenger trains from Northgate to Shotton, Wrexham and the Wirral ceased in September 1968, leaving only the former CLC service to Manchester which was diverted into Chester General via a modified connection at Mickle Trafford from October 1969. The line between Mickle Trafford and Hawarden Bridge remained open primarily to serve Shotton steelworks, latterly involving steel coil traffic from Ravenscraig in Scotland and returning empty wagons, until April 1984 when the line was closed and the traffic diverted via Wrexham. However, the requirement to work the loaded coil trains over the by then single track section from Saltney Junction to Wrexham, including the ascent of Gresford bank, and the need to reverse at Wrexham proved operationally impractical and led to a reprieve of the CLC/MS&L route which reopened as a single line in August 1986, making use of the best of the former double track by swapping between the former Up and Down lines in a number of places. Final closure came in June 1992 when, with the end of steelmaking at Ravenscraig, all Shotton's coil requirements were supplied from south Wales. After talk of part of the route providing the basis for a guided busway, it is now a cycleway and footpath – the Millennium Greenway – which forms part of Route 5 of the National Cycle Network.

162. CHESTER NORTHGATE, 1953
The approach to Chester Northgate Station, with the vehicular access gates still flanked by the original gas lamp posts, the left one has even retained its glass globe. Hardly a hive of activity, the taxi driver is probably just taking advantage of the refreshment room. Note the Union flag – this is Coronation Year.
[EC Lloyd Collection]

the railways of Chester and Saltney 109

163. CHESTER NORTHGATE, 1953
An inside view showing in more detail the double-trussed roof construction with smoke deflector channels above the platform lines and a train of typical CLC stock. [HC Casserley]

164. CHESTER NORTHGATE, 1950s
A view looking into the station showing the limitations of the covered area. The long platforms were no doubt provided to cope with excursion traffic. Former GCR/LNER C13 Class 4-4-2T (67433) awaits departure with an afternoon train to Manchester. [JA Peden]

165. CHESTER NORTHGATE, 1958
A view from the platform end, with a typical CLC timber signal box controlling movements. Note the bracketed advanced starting signal, the lower arm routes trains for the Wrexham line. [HJ Leadbetter]

166. CHESTER NORTHGATE, 1940s
One of the ubiquitous C13 tanks arrives at the head of a short passenger train, while another former GCR locomotive, a J11 Class 0-6-0, can be seen on the back road. Although notionally a freight engine, these and the earlier J10 Class were often seen on CLC local passenger trains. [Stephenson Locomotive Society]

167. CHESTER NORTHGATE, 1950s
Improved Director Class D11/1 4-4-0 (62665), *Mons,* seen on the stabling/run-round road. This was one of the second batch of the class provided with side windows instead of open cabs. [R Stephens]

168. CHESTER NORTHGATE, 1950s
A C13 simmers in the Wrexham platform, whilst a grimy unidentified Class B3 4-6-0 makes a spirited start with a Manchester train. [Milepost 92½]

169. CHESTER NORTHGATE, 1950s
This view, together with that in the previous photograph, conveys some idea of the platform lengths.
[R Stephens]

170. CHESTER NORTHGATE, 1949
Class C13 4-4-2T (67429) in early BR livery, brings in an ex-Wrexham train. [Lens of Sutton]

171. CHESTER NORTHGATE, 1949
D9 Class 4-4-0 (62305) passes the depot with a Manchester–Chester train. [Lens of Sutton]

172. CHESTER NORTHGATE, 1949
C13 Class (67414) is seen approaching the station with a local train. The depot coaling facilities are on the right and Chester South signalbox is visible to the right of the bracket signal. [Lens of Sutton]

173. CHESTER NORTHGATE, 1949
Chester South signalbox with C13 (67414) passing under the watchful eye of the signalman. The bracket signal has been cleared for a train to the Wrexham line, which can be seen diverging to the left. [Lens of Sutton]

174. CHESTER NORTHGATE, 1949
The early British railways livery is shown to good effect in this view of C13 (67429) departing for Manchester and passing the bracket signal seen in the previous photograph. [Lens of Sutton]

175. CHESTER NORTHGATE, 1949
A view of the northern, or steps, end of Chester South signalbox, with N5 (69293) shunting empty stock. [Lens of Sutton]

176. CHESTER NORTHGATE, 1949
D10 Class (62650), *Prince Henry*, waits to depart with a Manchester Central train. [Lens of Sutton]

177. CHESTER NORTHGATE, 1959
The influence of the London Midland Region can be seen in this 1959 view with a DMU at the Manchester-bound platform and a BR Standard Class 2-6-2T, with steam to spare, on a Wrexham train. [HC Casserley]

the railways of Chester and Saltney 117

178. CHESTER NORTHGATE, 1950s
Further evidence of the BR (LMR) with three of the Standard Class 2-6-2Ts in the station area. [JA Peden]

179. MICKLE TRAFFORD, 1950s
The first stations out of Chester to the east on both the former GWR/LNWR/LMSR joint line to Warrington and the CLC line to Northwich and Manchester are seen in this view at Mickle Trafford. The connecting line between the two was the subject of controversy over the years after a junction laid in 1875 was removed by the CLC in 1878 until finally constructed in 1942 for wartime strategic reasons. The CLC buildings are on the embankment are of timber construction, which was company policy in such situations.
[Stephenson Locomotive Society]

180. MICKLE TRAFFORD, 1930s
An early view of the joint line station before the link was made. The fact that no train is signalled to that platform obviously gives the station staff confidence to 'occupy the four foot' for the benefit of the cameraman. This would be anathema to the present day Health & Safety regime. [Authors' Collection]

181. MICKLE TRAFORD SIGNALBOXES, 1960s
This view, taken from the joint line, shows the two signalboxes at this location. The brick-built joint line box in the foreground was known as Mickle Trafford West, while the timber CLC box was Mickle Trafford East. The West box was opened in 1874 and had an 18-lever LNWR frame. The closure of Chester Northgate in 1969 required a remodelling of the junction to allow trains off the CLC Northwich line to gain access to the joint line and Chester General. The two pre-grouping boxes were replaced by a BR LMR standard box (with 35 levers) which was opened on 7 September 1969.
[T Bagley / J Penn Collection]

182. MICKLE TRAFFORD WEST BOX, 1960s
The signalman at the West box takes time out to pose for the photographer.
[T Bagley / J Penn collection]

183. CHESTER, LIVERPOOL ROAD, *c*1930
A panoramic view shows the lines to Northgate from Wrexham in the foreground, the through lines to Manchester in the centre and the goods yard at the rear. The station closed to passengers on 3 December 1951, but goods services continued until 5 April 1965.
[Stations UK]

184. CHESTER, LIVERPOOL ROAD, 1921
Chester Liverpool Road opened for goods traffic on 31 March 1890 as part of the Manchester, Sheffield and Lincolnshire Railways route from Wrexham to Chester Northgate and included a through connection to the CLC route from Manchester. Passenger services started on 2 November 1895, but the through platforms saw little use. The only timetabled trains were summer-only expresses between Manchester and Aberystwyth, which ran via Wrexham and the Cambrian Railways, route via Ellesmere, which were withdrawn after the outbreak of the First World War. This view shows a Great Central train from Wrexham to Chester Northgate, while the through platforms are occupied by private owner goods wagons. [Milepost 92½]

185. CHESTER, LIVERPOOL ROAD, 1950s
After 1965, the through line continued in use for freight traffic (mainly coal trains to Shotton Steelworks). Post 1980, the line saw steel-coil trains which travelled from Ravenscraig in Scotland to the finishing plant at Shotton. It closed on 20 April 1984 and the steel trains were re-routed via Chester and Wrexham. This proved unsuccessful and the line was reopened on 31 August 1986 and remained in use until final closure in June 1992. [D Giddins Collection]

186. BLACON, 1950s

The Manchester, Sheffield & Lincolnshire Railway, one of the constituent companies of the CLC, opened the Northgate to Hawarden Bridge line in 1890. From here the Wrexham, Mold & Connahs Quay line gave access to Wrexham. In 1897, the MS & L became the Great Central Railway, taking over the whole route. The first station out of Chester, heading west, was at Blacon, seen in this view. Both Blacon and the next station at Saughall boasted substantial buildings in a mock-Tudor style on the up platforms. [RM Casserley]

187. BLACON, 1960s
An ex LMS 8F Class 2-8-0 passes on the up line with a coal train for John Summers Steelworks. The modest waiting shelter on the down platform is a stark contrast to the splendid main building. [J Penn Collection]

Locomotive Sheds

188. CHESTER NORTHGATE CLC SHED
The small two-road shed at Chester Northgate was built within the goods yard on the east side of the station and opened on 2 November 1874. For most of its existence it was host to tank locos of various GCR and LNER classes, with larger LMS and BR standard types taking over in later years, and even a few BR standard tender engines being allocated in the 1950s. Its average allocation was a dozen locos and it closed to steam in January 1960, after which it became a DMU stabling point. This view shows the engine shed with Class C13 (5047) approaching. The pitched roof was removed and replaced with a flat roof in the 1950s.
[Stephenson Locomotive Society]

189. CHESTER NORTHGATE SHED, 1947
LNER N5 Class 0-6-2 tank (9340) stands outside the shed on 24 April 1947. The poor state of the roof clearly demonstrates why it needed to be replaced. [HC Casserley]

190. CHESTER NORTHGATE SHED, 1960
A view of the depot with its modified roof and an early DMU inside contrasting with the previous photo. [RS Carpenter]

191. CHESTER NORTHGATE SHED, 1947

The CLC route from Manchester to Chester was often the poor relation to the Liverpool route so far as motive power was concerned. Seen here on the coaling plant line is an elderly D6 Class 4-4-0 (2101) in April 1947, carrying the new number issued in the LNER's re-numbering scheme of that year. She was, nevertheless, withdrawn by the end of the year. [HC Casserley]

192. CHESTER NORTHGATE SHED, 1949
In contrast to the previous photo J10 Class 0-6-0 (65188) looks very smart as it displays its new British Railways livery. [Lens of Sutton]

193. CHESTER NORTHGATE SHED, 1950s
BR standard Class 2-6-2T (84001) is seen on the shed in the final years before closure. [JA Peden]

194. CHESTER, GWR LOCO. SHED, c1950s

The building which became the GWR shed was built in 1856 by the Birkenhead, Lancashire & Cheshire Junction Railway. It was a brick-built structure, 300 feet long, with a slate roof, and was located adjacent to the triangle of lines at the west end of the station. Access was off the Birkenhead line and was controlled by Chester No 5 box. When built, the shed had a 42ft turntable and a coal stage with water tank over it. By 1901, the shed had 57 locos allocated, which rose to a maximum of 65 in 1934. The shed was re-roofed in 1928 and mess rooms were added, while the coaling stage was protected from the weather with corrugated iron sheeting and a hoist and bucket coaling system was installed. Initially, the GWR had to share the site with the LNWR who had their own three-road shed. Disputes between the two companies led to the LNWR opening their own shed in 1870 at the east end of the station, with the GWR taking over the LNW shed from this date to increase capacity. This building survived until 1957, when it was demolished and replaced by a brick-built shed. The GWR shed closed to steam on 9 April 1960, with its remaining allocation transferred to the LNWR shed. It was then converted to a diesel depot with the first DMUs arriving in 1961. A former Midland Railway Class 4F brings a train of tank wagons off the Birkenhead line past the GWR shed, with a pannier tank and a prairie tank visible on the shed. [Milepost 92½]

195. CHESTER, GWR LOCO SHED, *c*1940s
A former LNWR Prince of Wales Class 4-6-0 passes with an incoming passenger train from north Wales. Pannier tanks are in evidence outside the shed. [Liverpool Locomotive Preservation Society]

196. CHESTER, GWR LOCO SHED, 1920
A driver poses outside the sheds with his Armstrong Class 0-6-0 (1111). [LGRP]

the railways of Chester and Saltney 129

197. CHESTER, GWR LOCO SHED, c1946
A dormant member of the 2301 Class 0-6-0 stands at the side of the shed. [BP Hoper/D Giddins Collection]

198. CHESTER, GWR LOCO SHED, 1919
GWR 0-6-0 (700) is another Armstrong design, but this version has a Belpare firebox. [LGRP]

199. CHESTER, GWR LOCO SHED, c1947
A view looking over Hoole Road bridge giving a more general view of the shed. The crew of County Class 4-6-0 (1029), *County of Worcester,* take a break from the footplate as they wait, presumably to take over a Paddington express which will have arrived from Birkenhead. [Milepost 92½]

200. CHESTER, GWR LOCO SHED, 1960
A view of the GWR shed shortly before its demolition. Diesel shunters occupy several roads, while a Matisa 'Neptune' track recording trolley is adjacent to the shed on the left. [RS Carpenter]

201. CHESTER, GWR LOCO SHED, c1950s
A busy scene as Stanier Class 3MT 2-6-2 (40084) passes the shed 'light engine'. An unidentified Castle Class 4-6-0 can be seen on the right by the coaling stage, while to the left, outside the shed, are a Hall Class 4-6-0 and a stationary boiler. [D Giddins Collection]

202. CHESTER, GWR LOCO SHED, 1960

Construction work is going on all round the 'new' 1957 shed in preparation for the changeover from steam to diesel. [RS Carpenter]

203. CHESTER LNWR SHED, c1920

The LNWR had to share the same site as the GWR and it was not long before the former were complaining of a lack of co-operation from the latter. The LNWR had no turntable and were supposed to use the GWR one, however this never happened as the two companies could not agree on charges for this use. Presumably the LNWR engines therefore had to turn on the triangle or else run tender first. By 1867, the LNWR had 55 locomotives based at Chester and urgently needed more accommodation. This, and the disputes with the GWR, drove them to purchase some land at the east end of Chester Station, between the Warrington and Crewe lines. A large eight-road shed, with hipped roof, was designed and opened in 1870, with access off the Crewe line and under the control of Chester Nº 1 box. When the LNWR opened a new shed in 1890 at Mold Junction, all Chester's goods locos were transferred there, leaving Chester to deal solely with passenger locos. The average allocation at Chester was 50, and it survived until 5 June 1967 when it was closed and demolished.

This rare print shows the access roads to and from the LNWR shed at Chester. Note the young 'spotters' on the embankment, obviously in more relaxed times.
[C Heywood Collection]

204. CHESTER, LNWR SHED, c1920
Another early view showing a line up of LNWR motive power. In the foreground is a 19-inch goods while the first two locomotives on the right of the shed are a Claughton and a 4-6-2 tank. [EC Lloyd Collection]

205. CHESTER, LNWR/LMS SHED, 1931
A display of LNWR motive power, showing (L–R) a Cauliflower, a 4-6-2 tank and a 19-inch goods.
[Gordan Coltas/EC Lloyd Collection]

the railways of Chester and Saltney 135

206. CHESTER, LNWR SHED, 1920
A superb study of LNWR 4-4-0 (1341), *Alfred the Great*, outside the shed with a footplate man just visible in the cab. [LGRP]

207. CHESTER, LNWR SHED, 1921
LNW 2-4-0 (1168), *Cuckoo*, is seen alongside the water tank. [LGRP/D Giddins Collection]

208. CHESTER, LNWR SHED, 1921
The crew of LNW 2-4-0 (1168) relax between duties. The loco's controls are clearly seen, along with the oil can on a shelf above the firebox door. The small circular number attached to the cab roof is the shed plate. [LGRP/D Giddins Collection]

209. CHESTER, LNWR/LMS SHED, 1935
The shed itself with all the doors open and the tenders of two former LNWR types facing out. [V Forster]

210. CHESTER, LNWR/LMS SHED, 1935
Another 1935 view at a busier time. Once again, former LNWR types dominate the scene. [LGRP]

211. CHESTER, BR (LMR) SHED, 1950s
A Class 4P 4-4-0 Compound (41157) carries its new pre-fix of '4' in the BR renumbering, but retains its LMS tender as it stands in a siding next to the water tower. [A Donaldson]

212. CHESTER, BR (LMR) SHED, 1950s
A former Midland Railway Class 2P 4-4-0 (40413) stands on one of the pit roads as a party of smartly turned out schoolboys pay a visit to the shed. [A Donaldson]

213. CHESTER, BR (LMR) SHED, 1950s
Another Class 2P (40628) is in charge of hauling the shed's breakdown crane. [A Donaldson]

214. CHESTER, BR (LMR) SHED, 1950s
The driver gives attention to lubrication of former LMS Class 6XP rebuilt Royal Scot 4-6-0 (46213), *The King's Regiment Liverpool,* in early BR days. [A Donaldson]

215. CHESTER, BR LMR SHED, 1967

Preserved Castle Class (7029), *Clun Castle*, stands alongside the water tank on the former LNWR shed in March 1967 after working a railtour from London Paddington. The shed closed a few months later. [D Gidddins Collection]

CHESTER, DIESEL DEPOT

This was based in the 1957-built shed which had formerly been the GWR steam shed. The first DMUs arrived in 1961 for local services, followed by locos for freight and express passenger services. A fuelling point was provided and the depot remained busy until 1990 when the DMUs were transferred to Longsight and Chester was left to handle a diminishing number of locos, as freight traffic declined and most passenger services were handled by DMUs. After privatisation, Alstom were given an order for Class 175 DMUs to handle most north Wales services. As the contract also included maintenance, Alstom took over operation of the depot. They decided it did not meet modern standards and was demolished in 1997 to be replaced by a new, steel-framed building which opened in December 1999, when it was renamed Alstom Train Care Depot.

216. CHESTER, DIESEL DEPOT, 1970s
A rather indistinct view of the approaches to Chester Diesel Depot with several DMUs and a Class 25 loco on the stabling roads. Chester Nº 5 box is on the right of the picture. [Pacer Archive Collection]

217. CHESTER, DIESEL DEPOT, 1980s
Locos of Classes 08, 25, 40 & 47 stand outside Chester Diesel Depot. A Class 47 stands alongside the fuelling point. [Pacer Archive Collection]

218. CHESTER, DIESEL DEPOT, 1980s
A Peak Class (45 104) stands at the fuelling point. While the pools of oil and grease show that diesels are perhaps not as clean as people think. [Pacer Archive Collection]

219. CHESTER, DIESEL DEPOT, 1980s
A large logo Class 47 dominates this shed scene while a DMU is visible in the background.
[Pacer Archive Collection]

220. CHESTER, DIESEL DEPOT, 1980s
Class 47 (47 347) stands at the fuelling point, with a Class 40 and a tank wagon in the background.
[Pacer Archive Collection]

221. CHESTER, DIESEL DEPOT, 1970s
Diesel parcels unit (W55995) on the sidings outside Chester depot. These units operated between Chester, Shrewsbury and Birmingham. [Ivor Martindale]

222. CHESTER, DIESEL DEPOT, 1970s
A single unit passenger railcar stands at the fuelling point in Chester depot. Many of these units were transferred to departmental use after withdrawal from passenger service. [Ivor Martindale]

223. CHESTER, GWR GOODS SHED, 1980s
After the closure of National Carriers Ltd in 1981, the sidings around the goods warehouse were used for stabling locos and stock. In this view there are DMUs alongside the building, while in front are a Class 47, with two passenger coaches, and a Class 08 shunt loco, with the brakedown vans. [Pacer Archive Collection]

Chester Wagon Works

Railway wagon repairs were undertaken at Chester almost from the beginning of railway operations until the final years of the twentieth century. By the 1880s there were no fewer than five works in operation. The LNWR had a small works opposite the main station building at Chester General (the connecting line for which crossed the station approach road). The GWR had a works at Saltney, while three private contractors – the Gloucester Wagon Co, the Midland Wagon Co and the Birmingham Wagon Co – operated at the west end of Chester General Station, in the area bounded by Brook Street Bridge and Black Diamond Street. A single works survived on this site until the British Railways era. The works closed in 1998.

224. CHESTER WAGON WORKS, 1980s
An exterior view showing the various types of vans and wagons that were dealt with at this location.
[D.M. Airey/J. Penn collection]

225. CHESTER WAGON WORKS, 1990s
In the period when British Railways prepared for a return to private ownership the wagon works adopted this symbol reflecting Chester's Roman heritage.
[DM Airey/J Penn Collection]

226. CHESTER WAGON WORKS, 1980s
Inside the works, most of the wagons on view seem to belong to the engineering department.
[DM Airey/J Penn Collection]

Signal Boxes

As Chester General Station grew, a number of signal boxes were built to control the various points and signals and, by the early years of the twentieth century, no fewer than seven were in use to control the complex layout. As they were such a prominent part of the Chester railway scene for over ninety years, it was thought appropriate to give them their own chapter.

CHESTER Nº 1, LNWR
Built in 1890 with a 60-lever frame, this box was was built in the angle between the Warrington and Crewe lines, at the east end of Chester General, to control the junction between the two lines as well as access to the LNWR locomotive depot. Unfortunately, it has not been possible to locate any photographs of this box, other than the distant view of it in photograph 4.

227. CHESTER Nº 1 BOX, *c*1960
In this view, the permanent-way engineers have taken possession of the Warrington line to renew some pointwork, while a passenger train is seen departing on the Crewe line. The new box is on the right of the track layout. This all-timber box was built to replace the previous LNWR box. Located to the north side of the junction adjacent to the Warrington line, it opened on 23 February 1958, with a 60-lever frame. It had a short life and closed on 16 September 1973 when its functions were taken over by Nº 2 Box.
[B Hikey/J Penn Collection]

228. CHESTER No 1 BOX, c1970
Seen from the opposite direction, the box oversees a DMU which is coming off the Warrington line with a local service, passing a new BR upper quadrant signal. The LNWR steam shed was beyond the road bridge, between the two lines. [EV Richards]

229. CHESTER No 2 BOX, February 1984
When it opened in 1890, this was one of the longest boxes built by the LNWR at some 96½ feet. It housed a 182-lever frame and was staffed by two men on each shift, routing trains into the various platform or goods lines. The imposing size of the box is evident in this view taken a few months before closure. The track in the foreground has been severed prior to removal. The new colour light signal on the left has yet to be commissioned, as indicated by the white cross. The cabinets to the right of the box house relays for the new power signal box. [C Wilson]

230. CHESTER Nº 2 BOX, February 1984
This interior view shows the impressive length of the box and its lever frame, and leaves the viewer in no doubt why two men were needed to operate it. [C Wilson]

231. CHESTER Nº 3 BOX, 1960s

Opened in 1890 with a frame of 45 levers, this was the smallest of the Chester boxes and also the most unusual, due to its location in the middle of the station, perched high up on top of one of the walls which supported the station roof. Its function was to control two crossovers between the up and down main platforms, enabling them to be split into two and thereby allowing the station to handle more trains and giving greater flexibility at busy times. The box closed on 7 December 1980 as part of the preliminary work for the re-signalling scheme. A close-up view of the box taken with a telephoto lens which must have been taken on a hot summer day as the signalman has opened the window at the left hand end of the box to get some fresh air. [EV Richards]

232. (BELOW LEFT) CHESTER Nº 3 BOX, 1950s
This view shows the LNWR bracket signal next to the box, with the passenger footbridge behind it. The only access to the box was from this footbridge. [EC Lloyd Collection]

233. (BELOW RIGHT) CHESTER Nº 3 BOX, MARCH 1969
A similar view to the previous one, but now the semaphore signal has been replaced by a colour light. [A Bodlander]

234. CHESTER Nº 3A, LNWR, 1950s

Opened in 1890 with a 79-lever frame, this imposing elevated structure was located at the west end of the station, adjacent to the up and down platform line which it controlled as well as the up and down goods lines and various siding connections. It did not control the main lines. It was replaced by a modern BR box in 1963. This view of the box taken from the up and down platform, showing the steep access steps to the box and Hoole Road footbridge beyond.
[EV Richards]

235. CHESTER Nº 3A BOX, LNWR 1960s

Castle Class (5025), *Chirk Castle,* arrives at the up and down platform, passing Nº 3A box. The point rodding descending from the box is clearly visible, as is the adjacent goods line which passes underneath the box.
[EV Richards]

236. CHESTER Nº 3A BOX, BR LMR, 1975
This view shows the second No 3a box which opened in 1963 and housed an 85-lever frame. It was built into the slope at the west end of the island platform and is viewed from the Down main platform, where Class 47 (47423) waits to depart with a Holyhead train. [HC Casserley]

237. CHESTER Nº 4 BOX, 1970s
Opened in 1904, Chester Nº 4 controlled the junction of the Holyhead and Birkenhead lines and dominated the west end of the station for eighty years. It contained a 176-lever frame and, like Nº 2 box, was double manned. In this photograph, the box dominates the skyline at the west end of the station, with the Holyhead line passing to the left and the Birkenhead line to the right. The diesel depot is playing host to various DMUs and a Class 31 locomotive. [Pacer Archive Collection]

238. CHESTER Nº 4 BOX, 1960s
This slightly more distant view shows the box framed by the impressive signal gantry that controlled the entrance to the west end of the station. The grandeur of the scene is only slightly diminished by the two colour light signals on the left. [HB Priestley / Pacer Archives]

239. CHESTER No 4 BOX, 1950s
A much closer view showing an earlier signal gantry which had been removed by the time of the later photos. The carriage sidings are well filled and a GWR loco is passing the box, probably en route to the shed. [I Vaughan]

240. CHESTER Nº 5 BOX, 1970s
This box opened in 1874 and was quite different in style to the other boxes, with a squat appearance and hipped roof. It is not known who built it, but the two large roof finials are in the style of the signalling contractors McKenzie and Holland, so they are the likely candidates for its construction. As the track layout expanded, the box had to be extended twice in order to accommodate extra levers, once in 1908 and again in 1915. In its final form it housed an 81-lever LNWR frame. Located to the east side of the Birkenhead line, it controlled access to the Great Western loco shed and the junction with the avoiding line. This photograph shows a view of the box looking towards Chester. The lines in the foreground give access to the loco depot while the Birkenhead–Chester line is to the right. [HJ Leadbetter].

241. CHESTER Nº 5 BOX, 1970s
The opposite side of the box with the CLC line to Chester Northgate passing behind the bracket signal on an embankment. The extensions were so well done that you cannot see the join. [HJ Leadbetter]

242. CHESTER Nº 5 BOX, 1970s
The signalman has time to relax for a few minutes in this view taken from the Cheshire lines bridge. The diesel depot is visible on the left with the Birkenhead–Chester line on the right. [B Hikey/J Penn Collection]

243. CHESTER No 5 BOX, 1970s
A view of the box taken from the entrance to the diesel depot with the CLC line in the background and two Class 47s about to come on shed. [Pacer Archives Collection]

244. CHESTER No 6 BOX, 1960s
Chester No 6 was opened in 1903 and housed an 80-lever frame, controlling the west end of the avoiding line plus various crossovers. It worked to No 5 box on the avoiding line and No 4 box on the main lines into the station. On the north Wales line it worked to Crane Street box, until that closed in 1967, after which it worked to the Saltney Junction box. When that box closed in 1973, No 6 took over control of the junction between the north Wales and Wrexham lines, a function which it performed until the advent of the power signal box in 1984. This photograph shows an ex-GWR pannier tank which has just come off the avoiding line, probably heading for Croes Newydd Yard at Wrexham or one of the Wrexham collieries, to pick up a freight. [Authors' Collection]

245. CHESTER Nº 6 BOX, 1968
A view looking towards Chester showing the extensive track layout controlled by the box. The two lines on the left are the up and down fast lines connecting to the new fork lines which were designated as up and down goods. The two middle lines are the up and down slow lines connecting to the old fork lines, also known as the up and down main. The line on the extreme right gave access to coal sidings. After the 1984 re-signalling there was significant simplification of the tracks in and around Chester. [Authors' Collection]

246. CHESTER Nº 6 BOX, 1957
Taken from a slightly different angle but from the same location as the previous photo. Prominent on the embankment to the right are two large telegraph poles with multiple crossbars. [FW Shuttleworth]

247. CHESTER Nº 6 BOX, 1960s
A close up of the box showing the detail of the supporting ironwork and the point rodding descending to track level. [HJ Leadbetter]

248. CHESTER Nº 6 BOX, 1960s
Viewed from the opposite side, the box stands out against a threatening sky. Note the entrance steps at the rear right of the girderwork. [HJ Leadbetter]

249. CHESTER POWER SIGNAL BOX, 2013

Plans for the modernisation of Chester's signalling system had been under discussion by British Rail since the 1960s, but it was January 1980 before a formal application was made to the British Railways Board to approve a scheme. This involved the complete renewal of all Chester's signals with colour lights controlled from a new PSB, together with considerable simplification of the track layout. The scheme was authorised at a cost of £6.8 million, with track and signalling work carried out by British Rail, while the new box was built by outside contractors. It is a rather anonymous building, located to the north-east side of the station, next to the goods warehouse. The work was completed in 1984 and the box was commissioned in stages between Friday and Monday, 4–7 May. A formal opening ceremony and dedication was carried out by the Bishop of Chester, the Rt Revd Michael Baughen on 12 June 1984. This photograph, viewing the PSB from the east end of the down main platform, shows it as a completely anonymous building which could be mistaken for a standard industrial unit. [A Bodlander]

250. CHESTER RESIGNALLING, 1984
After control had been transferred to the new PSB, the old boxes had to be stripped of their equipment before the buildings could be demolished. Here signal levers, point rodding, and other bits and pieces are piled outside Chester Nº 2. [D Giddins]

Bibliography

We make no apology for once again beginning with the relevant volumes of the *Regional History of the Railways of Great Britain* series (David & Charles), in this case Peter Baughan's *North & Mid Wales* (1980) and Geoffrey Holt's *The North West* (1978), as providing essential overviews of the development and operation of the railways radiating from Chester which have stood the test of time.

Turning to the individual lines which served Chester, most have been covered in some depth over the years. Probably the most extensive coverage is that of *The Chester & Holyhead Railway*, initially by Max Dunn (Oakwood Press, 1948) and subsequently by Peter Baughan (David & Charles, 1972), although sadly only the first volume of this history ever appeared in print. The story of the Great Western's route from Shrewsbury is a key element of Keith Beck's *The Great Western North of Wolverhampton* (Ian Allan, 1986) while the Birkenhead Joint was covered extensively by TB Maund in *The Birkenhead Railway (LMS & GW Joint)* (RCTS, 2000) and the LNWR route to Mold and Denbigh was the subject of Roger Carvell's *The Chester to Denbigh Railway* (Irwell Press, 2009). Moving to Chester Northgate, the Cheshire Lines Committee was still in existence when the first of several editions of RP Griffith's *The Cheshire Lines Railway* (Oakwood Press) appeared in 1947. Nigel Dykhoff has added to the literature with *The Cheshire Lines Committee – Then and Now* (1984) and *Portrait of the Cheshire Lines Committee* (1999, both Ian Allan). The Manchester, Sheffield and Lincolnshire Railway's activities west of Chester Northgate are covered in *The Wrexham Mold & Connah's Quay Railway*, by JIC Boyd (Oakwood Press, 1991).

Chester has featured in a large number of pictorial albums, of which two by SD Wainwright are worth seeking out – *Rails to North Wales* (1978) and *Steam in West Cheshire and the North Wales Border* (1981, both Ian Allan). Saltney's role as a centre for railway engineering is the subject of Tony Wood's *Saltney Carriage and Wagon Works* (Great Western Study Group, 2007) and a more general view of the Saltney area is given in *Railways around Saltney A Pictorial Record* by J Dixon and G Pickard (Geoff Pickard, 2006).

As with any part of the railway network, to understand how it really worked there is no substitute for studying the various official documents of the railway companies. One such volume which has been reprinted is the *LMS and GWR Joint Sectional Appendix to the Working Timetables for the Chester & Birkenhead and Shrewsbury & Hereford Sections* (Avon-Anglia, 1987). In addition, the chance find of a 30-page booklet detailing the arrangements for and content of a visit to Chester by the Chairman of the British Railways Board in June 1969 provided an interesting contemporary insight into how railway management saw their business in the immediate post-Beeching era.

Finally, the internet is the home of much fascinating material which although unlikely ever to appear in print, is nevertheless worth a look, although equally the ease with which material can be published on-line means that some of it must most certainly be taken with a generous pinch of (Cheshire) salt! Worthy of note are three websites in particular: www.nwrail.org.uk, a weekly on-line magazine compiled by Charlie Hulme; www.2d53.co.uk is Dave Plimmer's coverage of Chester and north Wales in the 'blue diesel' era of the 1970s; www.penmorfa.com presents Dave Sallery's personal selection from his photographic collection.